ORIGINS AND DOCTRINE OF FASCISM

ORIGINS AND DOCTRINE OF FASCISM

With Selections from Other Works

GIOVANNI GENTILE

Translated, edited, and annotated by
A. James Gregor

Routledge
Taylor & Francis Group
LONDON AND NEW YORK

First published 2002 by Transaction Publishers

Published 2017 by Routledge
2 Park Square, Milton Park, Abingdon, Oxon OX14 4RN
52 Vanderbilt Avenue, New York, NY 10017

Routledge is an imprint of the Taylor & Francis Group, an informa business

Copyright © 2002 by Taylor & Francis.

All rights reserved. No part of this book may be reprinted or reproduced or utilised in any form or by any electronic, mechanical, or other means, now known or hereafter invented, including photocopying and recording, or in any information storage or retrieval system, without permission in writing from the publishers.

Notice:
Product or corporate names may be trademarks or registered trademarks, and are used only for identification and explanation without intent to infringe.

Library of Congress Catalog Number: 2002021767

Library of Congress Cataloging-in-Publication Data

Gentile, Giovanni, 1875-1944.
  [Origini e dottrina del fascismo. English]
  Origins and doctrine of fascism : with selections from other works / Giovanni Gentile ; translated, edited, and annotated by A. James Gregor.
    p. cm.
  Includes bibliographical references and index.
  ISBN 0-7658-0130-2 (alk. paper)
    1. Italy—Politics and government—1914-1945. 2. Fascism—Italy.
  3. Fascism. I. Gregor, A. James (Anthony James), 1929- II. Title.

JN5450 .G413 2002
335.6'0945—dc21   2002021767

ISBN 13: 978-0-7658-0577-5 (pbk)

This work is dedicated to
PAOLINO LEONE
who died in battle at the age of eighteen.

Contents

Introduction to the Translations *A. James Gregor* ix

Origins and Doctrine of Fascism 1

What is Fascism? (Selections) 43

The Reform of Education (Selections) 77

Index 101

Introduction to the Translations

A. James Gregor

One of the better interpreters of the thought of Giovanni Gentile, Augusto Del Noce, identified Gentile's *Origini e dottrina del fascismo*, the translation of which is herewith provided, as a "document of major importance."[1] In Del Noce's judgment, Gentile's short exposition on its origins and doctrine was crucial to understanding Fascism's intellectual, emotional, and political substance.

Gentile's exposition in the *Origins* was clearly intended for an Italian audience.[2] As a consequence, the historic context behind his account is largely unknown to Anglo-American readers. Figures like Antonio Rosmini, Vincenzo Gioberti, and Ugo Foscolo are totally unfamiliar to an English-speaking readership. There is, perhaps, a vague familiarity with the name of Giuseppe Mazzini, but few could identify many of the tenets of his thought. Granted all that, knowledge of specific Italian literary, philosophic, and political personages is not essential in order to appreciate Gentile's account of the origins and doctrine of Fascism.

Gentile's claim is that Italy's involvement in the First World War was characterized by several important features: (1) it was initiated by a "directive minority" that succeeded in infusing "masses" with their conviction; and (2) it was not fought for the acquisition of material gain. Those claims set the stage for the further exposition.

The first contention reflected Gentile's considered judgment concerning complex political events. "History," Gentile was convinced, "is not made by heroes nor by masses; but by heroes who sense the inarticulate, yet powerful, impulses that move masses. [In the making of history] the masses find a person who succeeds in making explicit their obscure moral sentiments. The moral universe is that of the multitudes; and multitudes are governed and energized by an idea whose precise features reveal themselves to but few, an *elite*, who then proceed to inspire masses to give form and life to history."[3]

That interpretation of the dynamics of social change was shared by most of the significant social thinkers of the last quarter of the nineteenth and the first quarter of the twentieth centuries[4]—and Gentile was convinced of the merit of that assessment before there was an organized Fascism. He had expressed that characterization in his essays, written for more popular audiences, as early as 1918—before the manifest appearance of a Fascist movement.[5]

The second contention found in the opening pages of *Origini e dottrina del fascismo* referred to the common motive that bound together nationalists, revolutionary syndicalists, Futurists, and philosophical idealists. That motive, while "ideal" rather than "material," was not the defense of France or the United Kingdom—nor was it to protect "democracy" against the impostures of the "authoritarian" Germans and Austrians. The purpose of intervention in the First World War, "with or against Germany," was *the redemption of Italy*, begun with the Risorgimento, the nineteenth century effort to unite the Italic peninsula in a single nation. "Entry into the war," Gentile argues, "was necessary in order to finally unite the nation through the shedding of blood." Only that could create a "true nation," one that would "make itself valued and of consequence in the world." The purpose of Italy's intervention in the First World War was to finally participate in the making of history—never again to live "in the shadow" of others.[6]

For Gentile, the First World War brought into sharp relief the "two souls" of contemporary Italy, one that sought the continuation of the efforts of the Risorgimento, and the other that lapsed back into the behaviors of the "old Italy"—the Italy of empty rhetoric, passivity, egoistic amoralism, velleity, and anarchy. The first sought an Italy that was united and integral, that was "serious," with a seriousness that was religious in character, and infused with faith. It was a "soul" that sought the grandeur of the nation. Gentile identifies that "soul" with the thought of Giuseppe Mazzini.

In his exposition, Gentile seeks to establish a direct continuity between that thought, the Risorgimento, and Fascism. It was an effort that was to continue throughout the Fascist period, and found expression in the notion that the Fascist revolution was one that was "conservative"—preserving the revolutionary elements of Italy's modern political and economic developments of the preceding century in order to construct upon them.[7]

The effort was clearly designed to serve several purposes, one of the most important of which was to provide an answer to Benedetto Croce's claim that Fascism represented nothing more than a radical discontinuity in Italy's *liberal* political development. By the time that Gentile wrote the *Origins*, Croce had assumed an anti-Fascist intransigency, and his argument was employed to make of Fascism a meaningless "parenthesis" in the history of the nation.

Fascist intellectuals were to argue that Fascism drew on living elements of Italy's past—and was a perfectly comprehensible consequence of their accelerated revolutionary maturation.[8] Fascist intellectuals argued for continuity and anti-Fascists argued for discontinuity. It is a dispute that remains unresolved to this day. The notion that Italy immediately before, and certainly after, the First World War, was a divided, if not fragmented, nation is not in dispute. That there were "two Italies," one of which was "Mazzinian," and the other "anti-Mazzinian," was a common conviction. What is more interesting is the fact that Mussolini himself, apparently under the influence of Gentile, gradually accepted the distinction—and ultimately appealed to Mazzinian ideas to support his political positions.[9]

The "Mazzinian" ideas with which Fascism came to be infused were "Mazzinian" only in so far as Mazzini's ideas were interpreted by Gentile. Gentile saw in Mazzinian convictions philosophical idealism, a call to national mission, a consuming morality, a seriousness of purpose, religiosity, anti-individualism, totalitarian unity, an invocation to selfless duty, and the centrality of the state—all functional requirements for a nation undergoing late economic and industrial development in the early twentieth century, in an international environment dominated by hegemonic "plutocracies."[10]

None of this is difficult to understand. We have witnessed similar postures, political and social, assumed by revolutionary movements and revolutionary regimes in places as diverse as Eastern Europe, Latin and Caribbean America, the Middle East, Asia and, on occasion, in Africa. What distinguishes Gentile's thought, in some measure, is its insistence on *liberty* and *freedom* as the critical center of Fascist revolutionary thought.

Anglo-Americans have long suffered a curious intellectual affliction: they have been prepared to entertain a conviction that Marxist-Leninists—who have supervised some of the most thoroughgoing totalitarian political systems of the twentieth century—were nonetheless committed to a host of positive normative convictions such as equality, democracy, and freedom. They have *not* been prepared to consider the possibility that Fascist intellectuals held some of the very same convictions. Western intellectuals were prepared to argue that Marxist-Leninist intellectuals were betrayed by their leaders in the violation of equality, democracy, and freedom. They were *not* prepared to consider the same argument with respect to any Fascist commitment to such values. Marxist-Leninist intellectuals were betrayed; Fascist intellectuals were simply liars, frauds, and mountebanks.

The truth is that Gentile held *freedom* and *liberty* to be central normative convictions of Fascist doctrine. We may argue that such values were betrayed by Fascism, but we cannot insist that a case for them was not made by Fascist intellectuals. Gentile argued that the Fascist state was fundamentally *democratic* and predicated on *liberty*. For Gentile, the concepts were legitimately contested.

For Gentile, only when the individual fully identifies with the community, and its expression in the state, is *true* freedom and democracy possible. Like Marxist-Leninists, Gentile held that the individual is unreal, restricted, and unfree, outside the multiple relationships established in community with others. The individual for Gentile is, in essence, a *communal-being* (a *Gemeinwesen*). Full freedom and democracy for such a creature finds expression only in identity with the community (in Gentile's case, with the nation and its political expression in the state). How that identity is achieved is argued in Gentile's technical philosophical works.[11] For the purposes of the present rendering, Gentile provides a non-technical account in the selections herewith provided from his *La riforma dell'educazione* where the initial thoughtless "freedom" of students is reconciled with the "true freedom" of unity with the "authority" of informed instruction.

For Anglo-Americans, who have limited access to the Italian literature of the Fascist period, it is important to appreciate that Mussolini recognized that Gentile provided the normative rationale for Fascism and that whatever objections were raised, by both Fascists and anti-Fascists, Gentile's views would ultimately prevail. For Mussolini, Gentile was the philosopher of Fascism.[12]

Gentile provides an answer to the prevailing folk-wisdom of political science that Fascism was anti-intellectual, irrational, mindless, and inhumane. Whatever inhumanity, thoughtlessness, and perversity can legitimately be attributed to Fascism cannot be the consequence of the lack of a reasonably well-articulated and measurably persuasive normative doctrine. In dealing with Fascism as a doctrine, one can do no less than traditionally has been done with respect to Marxism-Leninism as a doctrine: one must consider it dispassionately and objectively in terms of the criteria employed to measure the credibility of *any* body of political thought.

The provision of a translation of the *Origins and Doctrine of Fascism* in its entirety, and selections from *What is Fascism* and *The Reform of Education*, are supplied as insights into the doctrine of Fascism, the debt of that doctrine to the thought of Giovanni Gentile, and the continuity of doctrine in time prior to the advent of Fascism. As has been argued elsewhere, Fascism grew out of the despair and humiliation of an Italy that had long been subject to the pretensions of the advanced industrial democracies.[13] It found its intellectual and normative rationale in the thought of Giovanni Gentile.

Some liberties have been taken in the translations, and no attempt has been made to preserve Gentile's singular literary style—sometimes baroque and sometimes synoptic. Rather, it is hoped that the translations are relatively easy to read and understand—and that they faithfully convey something of the substance of Gentile's ideas.[14] Inserts appear within brackets, and annotations appear in the endnotes with the intention to clarify or augment some matters that arise in the texts. Footnotes are presented as they appear in the original Italian.

Notes

1. Augusto Del Noce, *Giovanni Gentile: Per una interpretazione filosofica della storia contemporanea* (Bologna: Il mulino, 1990), p. 300.
2. Gentile prepared other works for foreigners, "The Philosophy of Fascism," herewith provided was one and the *Dottrina politica del fascismo*, prepared for the "Course in Fascist Doctrine and Activity for Foreigners" for the University of Padua, was another.
3. Giovanni Gentile, *Dottrina politica del fascismo* (Padua: CEDAM, 1937), p. 18.
4. See A. James Gregor, *The Ideology of Fascism: The Rationale of Totalitarianism* (New York: Free Press, 1969), chap. 2.
5. Giovanni Gentile, *Dopo la vittoria: Nuovi frammenti politici* (Rome: La Voce, 1920), pp. 5-8.
6. At the end of the Fascist experiment, Mussolini is reported to have said that Fascism was an effort to end "eighteen centuries of invasions and misery,...of servitude, of intestine conflict and ignorance." Benito Mussolini, *Testamento politico di Mussolini* (Rome: Pedanese, 1948), p. 33.

7. See Sergio Panunzio, *Lo stato fascista* (Bologna: L. Cappelli, 1925), pp. 21-30.
8. See Gioacchino Volpe, *Italia in cammino* (Rome: Volpe, 1973), pp. 7-24 and *passim*.
9. Del Noce, *Giovanni Gentile*, pp. 300, 330.
10. See A. James Gregor, *Italian Fascism and Developmental Dictatorship* (Princeton, NJ: Princeton University Press, 1979).
11. There are a number of works available in English that provide insight into Gentile's technical philosophy, included among them are H. S. Harris, *The Social Philosophy of Giovanni Gentile* (Urbana: University of Illinois Press, 1960); Roger W. Holmes, *The Idealism of Giovanni Gentile* (New York: Macmillan, 1937); Pasquale Romanelli, *The Philosophy of Giovanni Gentile: An Inquiry into Gentile's Conception of Experience* (New York: Birnbaum, 1937); and A. James Gregor, *Giovanni Gentile: Philosopher of Fascism* (New Brunswick, NJ: Transaction Publishers, 2001).
12. Del Noce, *Giovanni Gentile*, pp. 310, 312, 323; see Yvon De Begnac, *Palazzo Venezia: Storia di un regime* (Roma: La Rocca, 1950), pp. 540, 541, 619, 641 and Gisella Longo, *L'Istituto nazionale fascista di cultura: Gli intellettuali tra partito e regime* (Rome: Antonio Pellicani, 2000), chap. 1.
13. See A. James Gregor, *Phoenix: Fascism in Our Time* (New Brunswick, NJ: Transaction Publishers, 1999), chap. 2.
14. Two major works of Gentile are available in English: Giovanni Gentile, *The Theory of Mind as Pure Act* (New York: Macmillan, 1922) and *Genesis and Structure of Society* (Urbana: University of Illinois Press, 1960).

Origins and Doctrine of Fascism[*]

I. The Divided Spirit of the Italian People before the First World War

For Italy, its involvement in the First World War was the resolution of a profound spiritual crisis. It is from that reality that one must commence if one wishes to understand the slow and laborious maturation of some spiritual aspects of the nation's decision, in the first months of 1915, to enter into combat against the Central Powers, who at that point in time, were Italy's allies. From that point one can understand why the war had such singular moral and political consequences for Italy. The history of the war is not to be understood only in terms of a tissue of economic and political interests and military actions. The war was fought, first willed, then sensed and conceived worthy, by Italians: by a people composed of a majority led by a directive minority. It was willed, felt, and valued with such spirit that it could not be dismissed by Italy's statesmen and military leaders. They had to deal with it. More than that, the popular spirit influenced them and conditioned their actions. It was a spirit that embodied a sentiment that was not altogether clear nor coherent, neither easily determinable nor recognizable in general. There was neither unity at the outbreak of the war nor at its conclusion. At the end of the war, the different tendencies were no longer subject to the discipline which, during the war, had been imposed. That discipline was the result of the will of some, as well as the necessity of circumstances. After the war, there was no agreement [among Italians] because, to overlook the minor variations, there were in the nation's soul two distinct currents, representing essentially two irreducible souls. They had struggled for two decades, doggedly contesting the field, in the effort to achieve that reconciliation that seems to always require a war fought and a final victory—for the triumph of one. In such a contest, only the victors can conserve that which is salvageable from the vanquished.

---

[*] *Origini e dottrina del fascismo* (Rome: Libreria del Littorio, 1929).

One need only refer to the tortured history of Italian neutrality—to understand that there were not simply two political opinions or two historical conceptions that found themselves opposed, but two souls, each with its own fundamental orientation and its own general and dominant exigency. The enflamed polemics between the interventionists and those who chose noninvolvement, the different postures that the arguments of the interventionists assumed, the facility with which they accepted all the ideas, the most diverse and opposed, that were offered in support of intervention, and the means, of every kind, which the neutralists employed to defeat what they sincerely conceived to be the supreme tragedy of war testified to that.

For the one, the essential thing was to make war: with Germany or against Germany. To enter the war, to throw the nation, willing or unwilling, into the conflict—not for Trento, Trieste or Dalmatia, and certainly not for specific political, military or economic advantages that those annexations might provide, nor for the colonial acquisitions that others anticipated. These particular ends, of course, were to be taken into account. But entry into the war was necessary in order to finally unite the nation through the shedding of blood. The nation had been formed more through good fortune than through the valor of its sons—more the result of favorable contingencies than through the strength of the intrinsic will of the Italian people—a will conscious of itself, its interest in unity and its right to unity.

The war was seen as a way to cement the nation as only war can, creating a single thought for all citizens, a single feeling, a single passion, and a common hope, an anxiety lived by all, day by day—with the hope that the life of the individual might be seen and felt as connected, obscurely or vividly, with the life that is common to all—but which transcends the particular interests of any. The war was sought in order to bring the nation together—in order to render it a true nation, real, alive, capable of acting, and ready to make itself valued and of consequence in the world—to enter into history with its own personality, with its own form, with its own character, with its own originality, never again to live on the borrowed culture of others and in the shadow of those great people who make history. To create, therefore, a true nation, in the only way the creation of every spiritual reality is undertaken: with effort and through sacrifice. That which frightened the others—the wise men, the realists—was the thought of the moral risks to which the war would expose a young nation, never having been tested in a national conflict, not sufficiently prepared, neither morally nor materially, for such a trial, not sufficiently established in its structure to throw itself into a conflict that threatened the nation with collapse on the occasion of its first test. Among the wisest of the wise there was the calculation that neutrality in the war might produce more abundant benefits than victory in that war: tangible, determinate, material benefits, those which, for the pundits of politics, are the only ones worthy of consideration.

That was precisely the point of contention. The neutralists calculated, and the interventionists committed themselves to the war for an intangible, impalpable, nonmensurable moral concern—at least in terms of the judgment of others. That moral concern, however, proved to be more weighty than all the rest for those who accepted it. It is evident that calculations of advantage, of whatever order there might be, presupposes that there are those who profit, who are in a position to profit, and gain advantage. They defend and sustain all that as though it were important to one's selfhood. The fact is that the development of one's personality is the foundation and the principle of everything.

But everything can be nothing, for the individual and for peoples, without the will which can, and should serve, to make determinations of value. The will and the consciousness of self, character, individuality solid and powerful, are among the greatest riches that dying parents can leave their children, and which provides the inspiration for those statesmen who work for their people.

In the political conflicts before the advent of the Great War, Italy's duality of soul was manifest; one expression was to struggle against the neutralism of public opinion with ever-increasing insistence. The neutralists sought to resist involvement in the war not through the government, the center of legally constituted political power, but through Parliament. Parliament, at that time, seemed the source of all initiatives, the very foundation of the State. The Parliament became increasingly menacing and its behaviors more and more irreconcilable with the nation's executive, as though intent upon bringing the nation to the very threshold of civil war. That fratricidal war was avoided only through the intervention of the King, who provided the government the power to declare war.[1] That was the first decisive step toward the solution of the grave moral and political crisis [that characterized Italy before its involvement in the war].

II. The New Italy of the Risorgimento

The crisis of which we have spoken, had remote origins, with roots deep in the Italian spirit—a spirit of recent history, easily isolated, the end result of the secular development of its civilization. Italy's more recent history is that of the Risorgimento—the national movement of reunification of the nineteenth century—at which time this new Italy awakened and sought to arise and affirm itself. What were the active forces of the Risorgimento, together with the complex of external and internal conditions within which they were to operate?

There was the mass of the Italian people, to whom some historians today tend to attribute a notable if not predominate influence; there was English sympathy and French assistance; there was the war between Prussia and Austria, and between Prussia and France, and so forth, that could only but have impact on the Risorgimento. Without Cavour, Napoleon III would never have fought in Lombardy. But the primary causal agent is always an idea become person, with a will that pursues determinate ends—a cognizant will that has a program to realize, a concrete thought, effective in history. There is no doubt that the Risorgimento was the consequence of the labor of a few; and could be nothing other than the labor of a few. The few, in so far as they were the conscience and the will of an epoch, were the agents of history. They recognized the forces that were available, and employed that which was really the only active and effective force available to them—their own will.

That will was the thought of poets, of thinkers, of political writers, who at times know how to speak a language that resonates with a universal sentiment—capable of being its embodiment. From Alfieri to Foscolo, from Leopardi to Manzoni, from Mazzini to Gioberti they wove together a new fabric that was a new thought, a new spirit, a new Italy—that would distinguish itself from the old through a simple, but enormously important feature: it would take life seriously while the older Italy would not. Throughout history there was talk of immortal Italy; it was the subject of song; it was proposed in prose and in rhyme—with every form of argument. It always was an Italy lodged in the thought of intellectuals, and in doctrines more or less remote from life, in which those who take things seriously are required to draw out the implications of convictions and translate ideas into action. It was necessary that Italy descend into the hearts of Italians, together with all the other ideas relative to life's realities, there to become positive and vital elements. [To understand that is to understand] the significance of Giuseppe Mazzini's motto: thought and action. That was the greatest revolution anticipated and realized by him. He inculcated into many the conviction that only that thought which expressed itself in action was real thought. Those who responded—it must be remembered—were a minority—but sufficient to raise the issue where it could be publicly considered. Life was seen not as a game, but a mission. The individual has a law, a goal, through which he discovers his proper value, and for which sacrifice is necessary, with the individual forfeiting private comforts and daily interests, and, should it be necessary, his life [in order to reach that goal]....

No revolution displayed more of these features of idealism, of thought that preceded action, and its satisfactory outcome, than did the Risorgimento. It was not life's material needs or diffuse popular sentiments that erupted in revolutionary disturbances. The demonstrations of 1847 and 1848 were the work of intellectuals—as one would say today—and in the majority of cases, the result of the actions of a minority of patriots, who were the bearers of those ideals and who would move both rulers and the populace to their realization. There has never been a revolution, in that sense, that was more idealistic than that which fulfilled itself in the Italian Risorgimento.

Idealism is a faith in an ideal reality that must be sought. It is a conception of life that must not limit itself to present fact, but which must progress and transform itself incessantly in order to conform to a superior law that acts upon souls with the force of the soul's own convictions. Idealism was the very substance of the teachings of Mazzini.[2] That idealism, well or ill understood, was the spirit of our Risorgimento; and because of the moral influence which it exercised and the recognition with which it was received outside of Italy, revealed the historic character of that great event to the world. Gioberti, Cavour, Vittorio Emanuele, Garibaldi, and all those patriots who labored at the very foundation of the new kingdom were, in that sense, Mazzinians.[3] The entire Risorgimento was Mazzinian, not only in terms of the political forces in act, but in all the forms of the spiritual life of Italians, in which the influence of Mazzinianism matured independently of his writings and enjoinments. Writers of the first rank, like Manzoni and Rosmini, who had no historic relationship with Mazzini, shared the same traits, and on convergent paths, pursued the same end: to plant a conviction in souls—a conviction that life is not what it is, but what it ought to be; and only that life is worthy of being lived which is as it ought to be, with all its duties and difficulties, requiring always efforts of the will, abnegation, and hearts disposed to suffer in order to make possible the good—an anti-materialistic and essentially religious conviction.[4] One can run through the series of the writers and thinkers of the time. There is not a single materialist among them—not one who does not sense the religious character of life—who, irrespective of the political contrasts found between national aspirations and the dogmas and exigencies of the [Roman Catholic] Church, did not acknowledge, in some fashion, the necessity of reinvigorating the religious sentiment and revive in souls that faith, which for Italians had become no more than a formal and mechanical externality. Even Giuseppe Ferrari (who might be considered the exception) confirms the truth of the judgment—he who ultimately found himself in absolute solitude, opposed not only by Gioberti and the moderates, but by Mazzini himself. Ferrari was a restless, turbid, contradictory, inconclusive spirit, formidable in the brilliant quality of his genius and his vast culture, inept in his destructiveness, and incapable of construction.

The religion of Gioberti is not that of Rosmini, nor that of Manzoni. That of Mazzini is not that of Tommaseo, to compare spirits that shared affinities. Between Cavour and Ricasoli, who both keenly sensed the gravity of the religious problem—as a problem for both the individual and as a political problem for the new Italy—the difference is even greater. One of the thinkers more versed in religious matters is Lambruschini—who is studied even today with much interest for the freshness and profundity of his religious ideas, remains a solitary figure. In effect, one cannot speak of an Italian religious movement during the first half of the nineteenth century—a movement that had a character and a program, in which many participated. Nonetheless, at the bottom of all the variety of ideas and tendencies, there was a shared basis—a faith in the reality and the power of the ideal principles that govern the world. [It was a faith in which there was] a common opposition to materialism. That was the general character of the time. That was the ground on which everyone met and could agree or disagree.[5]

III. The Waning of the Risorgimento and the Reign of Umberto I

That religious and idealistic conception of life, which formed the basis of the national patriotic conscience of the Risorgimento, dominated and governed the spirit of Italians until its exhaustion as an historic movement. It was the atmosphere in which one breathed not only during the heroic times until the proclamation of the new Kingdom with Cavour, but also afterwards, in the period of the *diadochi*, from Ricasoli to Lanza, Sella, Minghetti, until the occupation of Rome and the establishment of the finances of the State,[6] until the time that the work appeared complete, the Risorgimento concluded, and the moment when the people of Italy, having become a nation through severe trials and hard discipline, were to be launched to democratically and freely develop their inherent economic and moral forces. The parliamentary change of 1876 signaled, if not the end, the arresting of the process with which Italy began the century—with that spirit we have attempted to describe.[7] The process was changed. It was changed not through caprice, confusion, or the weakness of persons, but as an historical necessity, that it would be foolish, today, to deplore. Rather, it behooves us to understand what transpired. It seems that liberty had been conquered, because from 1861 through 1876, Italian politics was directed by the Right, which was scrupulously concerned with statutory liberty—but which conceived liberty in a manner distinct from the Left. The Left moved from the individual to the State; the Right from the State to the individual. Those of the Left conceived the people—for a variety of reasons, and according to their origins and their different intellectual development—as the same as the citizens of which the "people" are composed. The Left made the individual the center and the basis of rights and initiatives—that any regime of liberty was required to respect and guarantee. The persons of the Right, on the other hand, as the result of various tendencies and modes of thinking, were firm and in agreement concerning the notion that one could not speak of liberty without speaking of the State. A serious liberty with important content could not obtain other than within the sound organism of a State, whose sovereignty would be the indestructible foundation of all its activities. The [State was understood to be the arena in which the] play of the interests of individuals is conducted. They possess no liberty worthy of mention that is not compatible with the security and authority of the State. The general interest is always to be given priority against any particular interest—to thereby absolutely and irresistibly endow the life of the people with value. A convincing concept, but not without dangers. Applied without regard to the motives out of which the opposed concept of the Left arises, and appears justified, it can result in stasis, immobility—and therefore in the annihilation of the life which the State embodies in itself and disciplines in the organic substance of its relations, but which it must not, nor can, suppress. [Only a State that responds to the considerations out of which the concepts of the Left emerge can remain vital and progressive. If the State fails to respond to those considerations] it becomes a form indifferent to content, alien to the things it must regulate; it becomes mechanical, and threatens to overwhelm those things with which it must deal.

The individual, in turn, who does not find the law within himself, does not become one with the State and opposes the State and the law. He senses the law as a limit, as a constraint, that would suffocate him should he not be able to free himself. That was the feeling of those of 1876. The people of the nation required more breathing space. Moral, economic, and social forces needed to develop without being further confined by a law that was not understood. That was the cause of the political change. From there our new nation entered into a period of growth and development—economic (industrial, commercial, rail transport, financial, and agricultural), as well as intellectual (scientific and scholarly), development. All to the credit of the reign of Umberto I. The nation that had received, as from on high, a form, arose, and made every effort to lift itself to a higher level, giving to the State that had already crafted its statutory codes, its administrative and political institutions, its army and its finances, a living content of real forces. Those forces grew out of the enterprise, both individual and collective, that were put in motion by the interests that the Risorgimento—all caught up in the grandeur of the political purpose to be attained—had not satisfied.

The most important minister of King Umberto, Crispi, aggressively sought to stop that movement of growth, to raise once again the flag of idealism—even religion—that he had been given in his youth by Mazzini, himself. He revealed a misunderstanding of his time, and fell before the violent reaction that the so-called democracy unleashed against his effort.

It was necessary, for the time being, to fold away the old and glorious banner. One was not to speak of wars, nor of anything that might signify and require national pride and consciousness of a program to be undertaken in competition with the Great Powers. One was not to dream of assuming any pretense of being on the level of the Great Powers or their proper equal. It was enough to participate in discussions with them, and return content that one's hands remained unsullied [by the acquisition of territory or resources so common among the "powers" at the end of the nineteenth century.] One was not to think of limiting individual liberty in the interests of that abstract and metaphysical entity that was called the State. One was not to call upon God (as Crispi was wont to do). One must allow the popular classes to gradually conquer well being, a sense of self, and enter politics. Education and the battle against illiteracy, together with all the other provisions of social legislation were to be undertaken. The removal of Church education and the introduction of secular public schools were sought.[8] There was everywhere and in every way a struggle against long-established and pernicious ecclesiastical influence, and the associations that arose to achieve that goal were to remain in Italy to pursue that end [at the beginning of the twentieth century]. Masonry continually penetrated, expanded, and branched out throughout the national administration and the military, into the magistrature and the schools.[9] The central power of the State was weakened, bent to the attitudes of the popular will by means of universal suffrage and the votes of parliament. That will was increasingly liberated from the limitations of the superior obligations of life....Less authority, more liberty.

The character of public life was shaped from below. And to increase the impetus and the force, there was socialist propaganda, of Marxist stamp, to which the rise and development of heavy industry opened the way. That was accompanied by a new form of moral education for the working classes and the formation among them of a political consciousness. It was a revolutionary consciousness, together with a sentiment of human solidarity, new to the primitive and unsophisticated psychology of the Italian lower classes. A new discipline came with the associations and federations of classes—but it was a partial and narrow discipline that limited the moral horizon and ruptured the majority of the ligaments with which the human being is morally connected to others. More than anything else, it did not allow the social awareness that draws human beings together in the service of interests, sentiments, and thought of a single Fatherland.

For the Left, the bonds that maintain and establish the community, which were conceived as respectable and to be respected, were all rooted in the sentiment that each instinctively has of conquering and defending his own proper well being—a *materialistic* conception of life against which Mazzini had struggled.[10] It was that conception that Mazzini opposed in socialism—but which he himself recognized was not limited to socialism, but was common to every political conception, liberal as well as antisocialist, that was democratically individualistic—in so far as life was conceived as devoted entirely to the satisfaction of rights rather than the discharge of duties. Liberalism and socialism are both individualistic in so far as both deny a reality superior to that material life which has its measure in the individual. Materialists are always individualists.

The Italy of the Left, from 1876 until the war of 1915-1918 was materialistic and anti-Mazzinian—even though it goes without saying that it was an Italy far superior to the Italy of pre-Mazzinian times. The light of the Risorgimento went out. Other than a few survivors, whose voices lost themselves in the desert, all of culture, in the moral sciences, as well as in the natural sciences, letters, arts, and education, was dominated by a crude positivism, which even when it protested that it did not wish to deal with metaphysics—seeking to remain in agnostic reserve—lapsed into materialism, conceiving reality as a finished something that limited and conditioned the lives of human beings, and which ultimately dominated them beyond every exigency and moral pretext. Morality was considered arbitrary and illusory. Everyone spoke of facts, of positive things. They ridiculed metaphysics and any reality that might be intangible. The truth was in the facts. One needed only to open one's eyes to see the mirror of truth in nature. Of God, it was said, it was better not to speak. Concerning the soul one might speak but only to conceive it as a physiological phenomenon which one might well observe. Patriotism—like all the other virtues that have their origins in religion, concerning which one could no longer speak unless one was prepared to speak with gravity—became simply an issue of inflated speech, which one ought to have the good taste not to consider.[11]

This—as it remains in the memory of those educated during the last quarter of the nineteenth century—was the spirit of that anti-

Mazzinian age, with the exception, once again, of a few faint voices, collected together in a common feeling. It was an age that could be politically designated a demo-socialist phase of the Italian State, because in Italy the democratic mentality found expression in socialism, an imposing and primary force. It was the age, as has been indicated, that filled the entire reign of Umberto I. It was a period of development and prosperity, in which the creative forces of the Risorgimento were overwhelmed and obscured.

IV. Idealism, Nationalism, and Syndicalism

During the final years of the nineteenth, and in the first three years of the twentieth century, youth found itself enveloped and transported by a new spirit, a forceful reaction to the dominant ideas in politics, literature, science, philosophy, and in the culture of the last quarter of the preceding century. Italy seemed fatigued, repelled by the prosaic, middle-class, materialist life that it endured. It was eager to return to its origins, to the ideas, the high aspirations, and the great moral forces that had given Italy birth. At the turn of the century, Rosmini and Gioberti had been generally forgotten. They survived only in cults having few adepts. Their books were rarely found in the bookstalls and among used bookdealers. Their names were barely spoken by scholars who had pretensions of being current. [By the first decade of the new century, however,] they returned with honor, and around their doctrines a new literature began to arise that saw in their thought something of great permanent value. The royal government itself decreed the publication of a national edition of the works of Mazzini. There was a return to the study of his life and writing, not only as a matter of historical interest but also as a source of instruction that could no longer be overlooked. Vico, the great Giambattista Vico,[12] the philosopher of the highest speculative national tradition, the formidable advocate of the anti-Cartesian idealist and spiritual idealist philosophy, was once again passionately studied together with other national thinkers. Italians could sense and reconstruct an autonomous and elevating consciousness of the proper personality of the nation. More recent writers (Spaventa, De Sanctis), who were not able, in life, to break through the resistance of those too obtuse to recognize the idealistic needs and the intimate intelligence of life and art, returned in honor, were republished, read, and universally studied.

Positivism, as it found expression in its major and minor representatives, was refuted—it was opposed, rejected, and satirized in all its forms. Materialistic methods of study in literature and art were fought, and discredited. The doors of Italian culture were opened to new ideas—ideas which, even beyond the Alps, substituted themselves for positivism and naturalism. The old Roman Catholic conscience was shaken, reawakened, and revived by the modernist movement that had been born in countries possessed of a more vital ecclesiastical culture.[13] It found ardent agents among young priests who, participating in the critical studies of the history of Christianity and the philosophic studies in which the movement found its origin, awakened among Italian clerics the need of a culture more modern and profound. They took effective part in religious controversies and struggles. They succeeded in bringing to light problems that had long remained in the shadow for Italians. Orthodox Catholics, modernist Catholics, and non-Catholics saw those problems with new eyes and more sensibility.

In the renewed philosophic and critical spirit, socialism itself no longer appeared to be a finished doctrine to be accepted as dogma. It was rather seen as a doctrine, like every other, that would have to be studied in its essence and structure. Italian scholars gave themselves over to the example and guide of the French, who had been dogmatic adherents of Marxism. Together, both the Italians and the French reviewed Marxism's weaknesses and errors. When Georges Sorel, as a consequence of that critique, defeated that materialistic theory of the German social democratic epigones of Karl Marx—and advocated syndicalism—young Italian socialists turned to him, and found in syndicalism two things: (1) the rejection of that strategy of foolish and deceptive collaboration of socialism with the parliamentary democracy of the liberal State. In so doing, socialism succeeded only in betraying the proletariat as well as the liberal State. (2) [As opposed to standard socialism, the proletariat found in syndicalism] a faith in a moral reality, exquisitely ideal (or "mythic," as was said at the time), for which one would be prepared to live, die, and sacrifice oneself, even to the point of using violence whenever violence was necessary to destroy an established order to create another. It was an anti-parliamentarian and moral faith that transformed the conscience of workers in syndicates, and made of the socialist theory of duties a Mazzinian conception of life as apostolic obligation.[14]

Another idea suggested by French culture—that had enormous impact on the youth of Italy and thereby penetrated deeply into the community, particularly among intellectuals, and which profoundly reformed political thought—was nationalism. Less literary and more political in Italy because closer to a political current that had an immense importance—the traditional Right—around which Italian Nationalism collected itself, emphasizing the ideal of the Nation and the Fatherland. It was emphasized in a form, as we shall see, that was not entirely acceptable to the traditional Right. The new form had to be forthcoming; one which advanced the conviction to which the Right had remained committed: to the State as the foundation in which the value and right of citizens was anchored. Nationalism, whatever the case, was a new faith lit in the Italian soul, thanks to which the Fatherland was no longer spoken of with socialist derision. The courage was mustered to resist the arrogance of socialists—that the liberals of various democratic persuasions found irresistible. Nationalism had another virtue: that of openly and boldly raising objections to that Masonry before which everyone in the Italian bourgeoisie had timidly prostrated themselves—save the Roman Catholics, who had directly opposed it. The anti-Masonic battles fought are among the signal honors of Italian Nationalism.

Masonry, parliamentary socialism, more or less reformist and democratic, became the common targets of the syndicalists, the Nationalists and the idealists: bound in a common cultural ideal and in a common conception of life. They had returned in unison, consciously or not, to a religious and idealistic Mazzinian conception. Separated by many of the articles of their special programs, they were nonetheless united and committed in that fundamental concept. They sought to infuse a consciousness of renewal and a vigorous sentiment of opposition among the youth [of Italy] against the prevailing culture and politics. During the first fifteen years of the century there was a ferment in newspapers, magazines, in the publications of the new publishing houses, and among the youth groups that had begun to organize. There was an emergence of new growth, of new forces, that turned to the remote past to recall to life the energy that would sustain hope for the future. They were innovators who made recourse to tradition. They were polemicists, sometimes violent, who advocated a system of order and restoration of ideal forces, in which everyone would have to subject themselves to the discipline of law. They appeared reactionary to the radicals, to the super-liberals of a democracy influenced by Masonry, and to the reformists of socialism. They were, rather, the heralds of the future.

Official Italy, legal and parliamentary, was opposed to them. The Italy of post-World War One had as its leader a person who possessed a secure intuition of collective psychology, an expert in the vices and virtues of the entire political and administrative mechanism in which anti-Mazzinian and anti-idealistic Italy had established and secured itself. He was skeptical or indifferent to high ideals, a simplifier of all the great questions, and a simplifier in terms of solutions. He was ironic, incapable of enthusiasm and grand affirmations for himself or for the nation that he was obligated to faithfully serve. He was a positive person, practical, crafty—a materialist in the Mazzinian sense.

The two antithetical currents that characterized pre-World War One Italy were identified with the names of Mazzini and Giolitti. The crisis that arose out of their mutual opposition was to be resolved only with the war. Only then was Italy to be freed of that dualism that wounded and paralyzed it—to create a unified soul and produce the consequent ability to act and to live.

V. The Post-War Prostration and the Return of [Giovanni] Giolitti

From the very beginning, the effect of the war was not what had been expected. The end of the state of war in 1918, released the people of Italy from the limitations and constraints of wartime discipline—releasing them to the freedom of normal circumstances. The right to free and open expression of their intentions was restored. Given the latitude made available by the renewal of parliamentary and popular liberty, the political and juridical order felt the weight of the popular will. Under that weight, the State gave evidence of unraveling—together with the moral forces that provided it support. Popular sentiment seemed to support the position of those who did not want Italy to enter the war—those who had done everything possible to impede that eventuality. It seemed that those so disposed were prepared to further test the already sorely tried nation and the limits of the State's strength. Popular sentiment seemed to argue that it had been unreasonable, arbitrary, and foolhardy to commit a young and poor people, not yet united as a national community, and without a military tradition, to the arduous challenge of international conflict. The socialists considered the expression of that sentiment a confirmation of their original position with respect to the war. They intoned hymns of victory and triumph. They felt that their resistance to Italy's participation in the Great War had been justified and the truth of their judgments demonstrated by the facts. At the end of the war, Italy's allies had turned their backs on her, minimizing Italy's sacrifice and the value of its contribution to the Allied victory. For Italy, justice would not be forthcoming.

There were Italians who perversely took pleasure in the frustration of the hopes of those who advocated intervention. They were not disturbed—as right reason would seem to dictate—by foreign malevolence. They seemed rather to welcome the abuse. There was an increasing appeal to democratic ideology toward which there had been far too much indulgence during the war. The intervention of the United States in 1917 brought with it the acceptance of a democratic ideology of the worst kind, that of Woodrow Wilson.

The Italian victory in the Great War was thus transformed into a defeat; and a sense of defeat diffused itself among the people of the nation: hatred of the war and of those responsible for Italy's participation in it. That hatred extended to the military that had served as an instrument in that war. There was hatred of that system that had made the war possible at all, by making Parliament (and what a Parliament it was!) unable to oppose it. In fact, the sentiment against the war was so emphatic that a minister of the monarch was found who proposed that the lower house of Parliament abrogate Article 5 of the Statuto, thereby making the declaration of war a prerogative, not of the King, but of the Head of the Government [the first minister]. With the unleashing of those singularly materialistic anti-national passions, there was diffused throughout the nation, together with an arch discontent, an anarchic disposition to undermine authority itself. The ganglia of economic life appeared thoroughly impaired. Work stoppage followed work stoppage. Its very bureaucracy opposed the State. Public services ceased or were disorderly. A lack of faith in the action of the government, and in the force of law, grew day by day. A sense of revolution permeated the atmosphere which the weak ruling class felt impotent to resist. Ground was gradually ceded and accommodations made with the leaders of the socialist movement.

The specter of Bolshevism loomed as a terrible menace. Giolitti—that execrated Giolitti of the beginning of the war, the "man of Dronero," who throughout the war was gradually forgotten by Italians, or who was remembered only as an exponent of that Italy that had died with the war—resurfaced. He was invoked as a savior. Under him, however, there was sedition among the employees of the State and the occupation of the factories by workers; the very economic organism of the administration of the State was mortally wounded. Those who had inflicted the wounds were treated with diplomacy—an open confession of the State's debility. Had Giolitti, thanks to the consequences of the war, triumphed over Mazzini?

VI. Mussolini and the Fasci di Combattimento

Under the government of Giolitti, however, the circumstances changed, and against the Giolittian State there arose others who were authentic opponents, those who had willed the war and had consciously fought it—those who on the fields of battle believed in the sanctity of sacrifice. On those battlefields more than a half million lives were immolated for an idea. It was they who felt how great a crime it would be if all that bloodshed would one day be seen as having been in vain (as their opponents anticipated). It was they who sought to kindle in the hearts of Italians, and in Italian history, the glory of the victory consecrated by the sacrifice. Among them were those magnificent men who had been mutilated, who had seen death up close, and who, more than other survivors, felt possessed of the right conferred on them by those many, many thousands, who had made the supreme sacrifice, to watch and judge the living. They, the mutilated and the dead, awaited that Italy for which they had been called upon to sacrifice and for which they had given their limbs and lives. They were Mazzinians, in effect, who had wanted the war, and who had gone to war, before all the others. They provided spiritual guidance and prompted faith in the youth of Italy. They found a powerful voice that gave precise expression, nobly and energetically, to their convictions, unconquered by the disillusionment and prevailing meanness of spirit. They found a man who spoke for all, who spoke above the tumult, and who made those listen who sought not to allow the precious heritage of the war to be lost. He was a man who understood how to speak to the heart, who roused and mobilized all the passions invoked by bloody trenches and victorious combat. [Those heroes of the war] saw shining as from a distant height, a burning will: that of Benito Mussolini.

Benito Mussolini had emerged from Italian socialism in 1915 in order to become a more faithful interpreter [of the will of] the people of Italy, to whom he, already editor of the socialist paper, *Avanti!*, wished to devote his new journal, *Il popolo d'Italia*. He argued for the necessity of the war, for [Italy's entry into] which he was among those truly responsible. Just as he had struggled against Masonry while a socialist, inspired by Sorellian syndicalism, he opposed the parliamentary corruption of reformism with the idealistic postulates of revolution and violence in the name of revolution. Outside the ranks of official socialism, he continued his battle against his old comrades, defending the rationale of the war, defending the infrangible moral and economic wholeness of the national organism, against the lying fictions of internationalism. He argued for the sanctity of the Fatherland—[something that would be sacred] even for the working classes. He was a Mazzinian with the sincerity that Mazzinianism always found in Romagna. He had already transcended the ideology of socialism—first by instinct and then by reflection. Having passed through a painful and troubled youth, rich with experiences and meditation, he had nurtured himself with the most recent [anti-positivist and anti-materialist] culture of Italy. [He gave himself over to the concept of] that great Italy, which he—together with all those young men who, throughout the war—longed for and passionately loved. All had grown with the new ideas of the century, and in the new faith in the ideal—against the demagogic and anarchist velleities of those socialists who preached revolution with neither the force nor the will to undertake it. [Those failed socialists were persons who] even on the most propitious occasions failed to recognize the necessity of assuring the most essential condition for the existence of a nation: a State form that would be truly a State, with a law to be respected, with an authority that made itself respected, possessed of a worth that would legitimate that authority. A nation—that was capable of sustaining a war that was in every way arduous, long, and bloody—a nation continuously victor over itself, tenacious in controlling the forces in act, making sacrifices in the constancy of a faith perpetually renewed, irrespective of deficiencies, disappointments, and tremendous reversals, achieving victory, in effect, through its own virtue—could be thrown into disorder and degradation without the respect and authority required by the State. The debasement of the State was accomplished by a few men like Treves, Turati, and their like—men without faith, political aesthetes, with all the brilliant culture of journalists, together with arid and empty hearts. On the 23rd of March of 1919, in Milan, at the site of Mussolini's newspaper, *Il popolo d'Italia*, the first Fascio di Combattimento was founded. In response to the will of its Leader—the destructive and negative post-war movement [in Italy] was soon to be halted. The Fascists called together those Italians who—the disappointments and the anguish that came with peace notwithstanding—continued to have faith in what the war, and what the victory in that war, meant. They sought to restore Italy to itself, through the reestablishment of discipline and the reordering of social and political forces within the State. Fascism was not an association of believers, but a party of action, that had need not of programs of particulars, but of an idea, that indicated a goal, and thereby a way to be followed with a resolute will—that refused to acknowledge obstacles, because ready to overcome them.

Was that will *revolutionary*? Yes, because it anticipated the construction of a new State.

VII. Redemption

The twenty-third of March 1919 was the date when the redemptive counteroffensive began—when out of Milan a cry was raised that awakened the spirit of the veterans who had wanted the war and who had fought it—who had sensed its value, and who had faith in their idea, notwithstanding the frustrations of a peace that was neither glorious nor just, and notwithstanding the vile spectacle of an ignorant people swept up in the arrogance of skeptics. The skeptics had been negative on the eve of the war; they opposed the war during the long, dark, and anxious days of trial, and they denied it, with malign smiles, after victory bore little fruit and reward. After the victory, they continued to maintain that the carnage was pointless, and those who had willed the war were to be deplored, scorned, and persecuted. Those who had worked for the victory were despised and derided. The spirit of the nation was prostrate. The consciousness of the sanctity of the nation—of the will that governed it, of the law that was its essence and which took form in a living person—was lost. The least noble passions of humankind were released and stirred. A revolution threatened that was without ideas or energy. It had bred during the long postwar inertia—like disease bacteria—that undermined the living body from within. It was a potential revolution without the strength of revolution, without the ability to destroy in order to create. It was a negative revolution. It was said that it was Bolshevik—but it was worse than Bolshevik. Against that revolution the veterans arose, mobilized by that powerful cry that in 1915 had given expression to their faith and had nourished it thereafter. They collected themselves in *Fasci*, associations that quickly multiplied throughout the nation.

And those associations made a revolution: a revolution that was possessed of an idea, a will, and a Leader. It had all begun with the war, declared in a manner that had already mortally wounded the Parliament, reducing to rubble the legal objections that obstructed the realization of the profound national will of a people who sought the dignity and power of their nation.

That revolution was undertaken and pursued with energy until the goal was attained. The illegalities of the four-year period (1919-1922) constituted the necessary condition for the manifestation of the national will—until the 28th of October 1922, when the old State was brushed aside by the impetus of the new youthful faith, and the *Fasci* became the new Italy.

From that day, the new nation reconstructed itself, because that powerful cry had by that time awakened all Italians, and animated and guided them in their arduous labor.

VIII. Squadrism

The four year period 1919-1922 was characterized, in the development of the Fascist revolution, by the deployment of Fascist squads. The action squads were the military force of a virtual State. [They were the military arm of a State] in the process of realizing itself—which in order to create a superior regime, violated the controlling laws of a moribund State system— understood as inadequate to the demands of the national State sought by the revolution. The March on Rome of the 28th of October 1922 was not the beginning, but the conclusion of that revolutionary movement, which on that date, with the consequent constitution of the Mussolini ministry, assumed full legality. From that point, Fascism, as the directive idea of the State, underwent evolution, slowly creating the institutions necessary for its actuation and its investment of all the economic, juridical, and political arrangements which make up the State, and which the State guarantees.

After the 28th of October 1922, Fascism no longer confronted a State that was to be destroyed; Fascism became the State and proceeded against those internal factions that opposed and resisted the development of those Fascist principles that were expected to animate the new State. Fascism was no longer a revolution against the State, but a revolutionary State mobilized against the residue and internal debris that obstructed its evolution and organization. The period of violence and revolutionary illegality had ended—although the activity of the squads continued for a time to flicker here and there—in spite of the iron discipline imposed by the Duce of Fascism and Head of the Government. Mussolini sought to have reality conform to the logic that governed the development of his idea and that of the Party that incarnated that idea. Fascism possessed all the means necessary for reconstruction: it transformed its own illegal action squads into the legal voluntary militia—in which the spirit of the revolution would be maintained until the fulfillment of the revolutionary program.[15] The Party was established in an inflexible and perfect hierarchy obedient to the intentions of its Leader, and was rendered an instrument of government action, ready, with spirit, to face the test. The Italy of Giolitti was finally overcome, at least in the realm of armed politics. Between Giolitti and the new Italy—the Italy of the combat veterans, of the Fascists, and believing Mazzinians—flowed a river of blood. That torrent barred the way to anyone who advocated turning back. The crisis was transcended, and the war began to bear fruit.

IX. The Totalitarian Character of the Doctrine of Fascism

The history of the Italian spiritual and political crisis and its solution was immanent in the concept of Fascism. How the legislative and administrative actions of the revolutionary government dealt with that crisis is not the present object of discussion. Rather, the present account is intended to illuminate the spirit which the government brought to its activities—which, in five years, profoundly transformed the nation's laws, orders, and institutions—thereby revealing the essence of Fascism.

It has already been said that before the complexity of the movement, nothing is more instructive for understanding it than, as we have already indicated, to consider Mazzini.[16] His conception was a political conception—a conception of integral politics, a notion of politics which does not distinguish itself from morality, from religion, or from every conception of life that does not conceive itself distinct and abstracted from all other fundamental interests of the human spirit. In Mazzini, the political man is he who possesses a moral, religious, and philosophical doctrine. Should one endeavor to separate, in Mazzini's creed and in his propaganda, that which is merely political from that which is his religious, his ethical intuition, moral enjoinments, his metaphysical convictions, one can no longer account for the great historical importance of his belief system and his propaganda. One can no longer understand the reasons why Mazzini attracted so many to himself—and proceeded to disturb the sleep of so many men of State and of the police. The analysis that does not always presuppose a unity [at the base of Mazzini's thought], does not lead to a clarification, but rather to a destruction of those ideas that exercised such historic consequences. It is evidence that human beings do not deal with life in slices, but rather as an indivisible unity.

The first point, therefore, that must be established in a definition of Fascism, is the totalitarian character of its doctrine, which concerns itself not only with political order and direction of the nation, but with its will, thought and sentiment.

X. Thought and Action

The second point. The doctrine of Fascism is not a philosophy in the ordinary sense of the term, and still less is it a religion. It is also not an explicated and definitive political doctrine, articulated in a series of formulae. The truth is that the significance of Fascism is not to be measured in the special theoretical or practical theses that it takes up at one or another time. As has been said at its very commencement, it did not arise with a precise and determinate program. Often, having settled on an immediate goal to be attained, a concept to be realized, a course to be followed, it has not hesitated, when put to the test, to change direction and reject as inadequate, or violative of principle, just that goal or that concept. Fascism sought not to bind the future. It has often announced reforms that were politically opportune, but the announcement itself did not bind the regime to their execution. The real commitments of the Duce are always those that are formulated and undertaken at one and the same time. For that reason Mussolini has always considered himself a "tempist," that is to say a person who undertakes a solution and acts at that proper moment in which action finds all the conditions and reasons mature that render the action possible and opportune. Fascism draws out of the Mazzinian truth, *thought and action*, its most rigorous significance, identifying the two terms in order to have them perfectly coincide, no longer to attribute any value to thought that is not translated or expressed in action. That is the source of all the expressions of "anti-intellectualist" polemics that constitutes one of Fascism's most recurrent themes. It is a polemic that is eminently Mazzinian, because "intellectualism" [as "intellectualism" is understood by Fascists] divorces thought from action, science from life, the brain from the heart, and theory from practice. It is the posture of the talker and the skeptic, of the person who entrenches himself behind the maxim that it is one thing to say something and another thing to do it; it is the utopian who is the fabricator of systems that will never face concrete reality; it is the talk of the poet, the scientist, the philosopher, who confine themselves to fantasy and to speculation and are ill-disposed to look around themselves and see the earth on which they tread and on which are to be found those fundamental human interests that feed their very fantasy and intelligence. "Intellectuals" are all those who represent that old Italy. They were the enemy of Mazzini's heated preachments.

Anti-intellectualism does not mean, as some ignorant Fascists seem to believe, that they are authorized by the Duce to dismiss science and philosophy. It does not mean that one denies the value of thought and those superior expressions of culture through which thought expresses itself. Spiritual reality is a synthesis, in whose unity one finds expression and value in that thought that is action. In the conclusive unity of that synthesis converge, and must converge, and know that they converge, many elements without which the synthesis would be empty, operating in a void. Among these elements are all the forms of spiritual activity, which share in the same value which is that of the synthesis. All the elements of the synthesis are essential. One does not rout armies that threaten the Fatherland with trigonometry—but without trigonometry one cannot target artillery. Anti-intellectualism is directed against those human beings who exhaust their spiritual life in an abstract and remote intellectual activity, far from that reality, in which everyone should realize that human existence is rooted. Anti-intellectualism is opposed to those postures that are sometimes assumed that miss superior, more concrete, more humane alternatives. The adversary that first of all is to be defeated is that adversary found among those that are mentally, morally, and historically, typical of that cultivated Italian class, that have been identified for centuries as *literati*. That would include not only authors and cultivators of literature, but every writer, even those writing about science and philosophy, even those who would occupy themselves with liberal studies—that is to say, even those disinterested and nonprofessional—academics, who are erudite, scholars, who would not involve themselves in politics, in real matters, those who would not involve themselves in the practical world. Such persons are the bastard product of our Risorgimento—whom Fascists justly consider bad citizens—the products of a growth which Fascists seek to extirpate.

Such an anti-intellectualism does not imply a hostility to culture, but a hostility to a decadent culture. It is hostile to that culture that does not educate and which does not make, but rather unmakes, the person, rendering him a pedant, an intellectual aesthete. The person is rendered an egoist, a man morally and therefore politically indifferent—one who considers himself superior to the fray, even when the struggle involves his Fatherland—even when interests that should win because their triumph signals the victory of his own and the defeat of enemies. Human beings make progress by dividing themselves through victory in battle and in the success of the one above the other. Woe to those who do not participate in the service of either side, and fail to commit themselves, remaining aloof, conceiving duty to be that of a spectator, awaiting an outcome and taking advantage of it, at the close of a conflict, waiting to partake of the fruits of the victor. The intellectualist sees the summit of wisdom in achieving that state of apathy in which one can consider the pros and cons of everything, extinguishing every passion, finding a place where he might watch, with security, those who suffer and die. But that is the epicurean ideal. All of human history opposes itself to that kind of epicureanism. Human history, heavy with everything we hold dear, in which, and for which, we live, is strewn with trials.

Because of its repugnance to that kind of intellectualism, Fascism is not enamored of tarrying in the making of abstract theories—not because it does not allow the making of theory, but because it does not expect theory to serve as a major force for the reform or the promotion of Italian culture and life. On the other hand, when it is said that Fascism is not a system or a doctrine, one must not imagine that Fascism is empty of reason, is blind practice, or a method that is indefinable or instinctive. Rather, if one defines as system or philosophy something alive, as a principle of universal character in its very development, a principle capable of revealing, as it develops literally day by day, its creativity together with the results and consequences of which it is capable, Fascism is a perfect system, with a most steadfast principle possessed of a rigorous logic of development. The Duce himself, together with the most humble member of the Party, recognizing the truth and the vitality of that principle, labor for its development, now moving with security along the direct route to the goal, and at other times making and unmaking, now moving forward and at other times returning to the beginning out of commitment to the logic of development—because some effort revealed itself as failing to accord itself with principle.

In that sense—as an open system dynamically capable of development—there is philosophy in every great body of thought, be it a political or social revolution, or a religious reform, or as a moral or critical literary movement. In this sense, the thought of Mazzini is a philosophy, as is the thought of Manzoni, as is that of Pascal as well as Goethe, Leopardi, and as is the thought of Byron or Shelley.[17]

None of these belong to the proper history of philosophy, but each belongs to a philosophical current, and they reject all that which deviates or contradicts it. If one fails to understand this, one could not identify or evaluate Fascism. One might consider Fascism a method, more than a philosophical system, because in ordinary language the term system is understood to mean a developed doctrine containing theories fixed in propositions or theorems to which nothing can be added and nothing subtracted. Nothing could be more alien to Fascism than those philosophic or religious doctrines which implicitly entail the rise of a school or sect, with adepts and heretics.

XI. The Center of the System

The third point. The Fascist system is not a system, but has in politics, and in the interest of politics, its center of gravity. Born as a conception of the State, intended to resolve the political problems exacerbated in Italy by the release of the passions of the unthinking masses of the post-World War I period, Fascism took the field as a political method. But in the act of confronting and resolving political problems, Fascism, in accordance with its very nature, by its very method, posed for itself moral, religious, and philosophical problems—and, in so doing, developed and demonstrated its specific totalitarian character. That provided the occasion for putting the political form of its principle to the fore. In manifesting that principle, Fascism revealed its specific content—without immediately revealing its ideal origins in a more profound intuition of life, from which the political principle arises. This allows us to outline a rapid synthesis of the political doctrine of Fascism, which does not exhaust its content, but which constitutes that part, or better that preeminent, and generally most interesting, expression.

XII. The Fascist Doctrine of the State

Fascist politics turns entirely on the concept of the national State—a concept which has many points of contact with the doctrine of Nationalism—so many points in fact, that it permitted the fusion of the Nationalist Party with that of Fascism in a single program. Nonetheless, the Fascist concept has its proper character. That cannot be overlooked. Without recognizing that, one would neglect that which is peculiar and characteristic of Fascism. Comparisons are never very generous—still less the one here proposed. Nonetheless, the effort will be undertaken to bring to light the essence of Fascism.

Both Nationalism and Fascism place the State at the very foundation of every individual value and right. For both, the State is not a consequence, but a beginning. The relationship between the individual and the State proposed by Nationalism was the direct antithesis of that advanced by individualistic liberalism and socialism. For Nationalists, the State is conceived as prior to the individual. For liberals and socialists, on the other hand, the individual is understood to be something that precedes the State, who finds in the State something external, something that limits and controls, that suppresses liberty, and that condemns him to those circumstances into which he is born, circumstances within which he must live and die. For Fascism, on the other hand, the State and the individual are one, or better, perhaps, "State" and "individual" are terms that are inseparable in a necessary synthesis.

Nationalism, in fact, bases the State on the concept of the nation—an entity that transcends the will and the personality of the individual because it is conceived as objectively preexistent, independent of the consciousness of individuals. Individuals do not labor to create it. The nation of the Nationalists is something that exists not because of spiritual activity, but as an empirical fact and a datum of nature. The constituent elements that make up the nation are territory or ethnicity—all of the same extrinsic nature, even when they are human in origin, like language, religion, or history. That is because those human elements that combine to create national individuality preexist, and the individual finds them already in existence, until he initiates that moral activity that engages and develops them. Much the same can be said of territory and ethnicity. Naturalism, is the disability that attends the tendentially spiritualistic thrust of Nationalism, and makes of it something inflexible, illiberal, retrograde, and crudely conservative—its least sympathetic element. Before Fascism—with which it was later to assimilate and amalgamate—that flaw made it suspicious and repugnant even to those who politically sympathized with most of its postulates. On the other hand, it attracted certain mysticoreligious attachments that proved to be one of the most effective reasons for the enthusiastic adherence to Nationalist idealism by the youth of Italy and those intellectuals not given to political reflection.

One of the special and conspicuous reflections of naturalism was the monarchial loyalty of the Nationalists. The monarchy was a presupposition for them. The Italian State had been born with its monarchy and by virtue of that, the historic basis that today constitutes Italian nationality includes the monarchy. It is a history that intimately and indissolubly binds a people together. There are the Alps and the Appenines, there is Sicily and Dalmatia, there is the undertaking of The Thousand of Garibaldi, and there is the House of Savoy. With the subtraction of any of these elements, one would no longer have the nation. To agree with that, as one must, is to consent to those elements—to feel them as inseparable from the very personality of being Italian. [For the Nationalists] it is not consciousness, recognizing and feeling the tie or rapport that creates and confers upon them the moral value and the obligation they are due, but it is the natural or historical connection and rapport that preexists, that determines the appropriate consciousness. That consciousness is virtually the product of those preexisting natural elements.

When Fascism sought its own path, on the other hand, it was acutely aware of the tedium and dissatisfaction with the actual political State of the Italian nation. Fascism was not capable of persuading itself that the monarchy could, with a vigorous effort, energetically react to restore the nation to that path clearly designated by the generous sacrifices of the war and by the victory honorably concluded. Fascism could not imagine what roots that monarchy could have, and maintain, in the reality that was the Italy of Vittorio Veneto. For that reason, Fascism did not hesitate to frankly confess a republican tendency. Later, when Vittorio Emanuele refused to invoke that state of siege proposed by the last prime minister of the old regime against the Fascist March on Rome, and chose to resolve the crisis between the old and the new Italy, as in 1915, by assigning power to the new Italy—resolutely violating the customary norms of the parliamentarianism responsible for the grave crisis—that antimonarchial disposition did not impede Mussolini from taking an oath of fealty to the King, thereby breaking definitively, sincerely and logically from republicanism. That signified that Fascism, unlike Nationalism, saw in the monarchy not the past to be respected as an historic fact, but as something alive in the soul, a future to which the spirit turns as to a proper ideal, an ideal that addresses our aspirations, our needs, our nature.

The monarchy, as with all the determinations of the State, as the State, is not something delivered to us by history; neither is it outside of us. The State is within us, mature, alive and of necessity living and growing and expanding and elevating itself in dignity, and conscious of itself and of its high duties and the grand goals to which it is called, in our will, in our thought, and in our passions. The individual develops and the State develops. The character of the individual consolidates itself, and with that character, the structure, the force, and the efficacy of the State consolidates itself.

Italy's seas, coasts, and mountains seem to acquire more cohesion and integrity as though they were ideas and sentiments. Everything in nature can be divided and disaggregated if it pleases us, or at least does not displease us—and everything can be rendered one and indivisible, if we feel that unity to be necessary. Past history with its memories and traditions, with its vanity and its titles to glory, is reconstituted and finds a place through our interested and fervid spiritual reinvocation. It is the spirit which makes them its own, to support and defend them with its adhesion and vigilant consciousness. The language of our fathers is enjoyed and appropriated— and it revives, being studiously taken in and savored with all its expressive qualities. It had seemed as though all that had preexisted—an hereditary legacy—but in fact it is transfigured in our own personal conquest and in a continuous creation, that would vanish if we failed to understand that we are its author.

XIII. The Fascist State as a Democratic State

The Fascist State, therefore, as distinct from the Nationalist State, is an entirely spiritual creation. It is a national State, because from the point of view of Fascism, it is the result of spiritual action rather than a presupposition. The nation is never complete—nor is the State simply the nation in its concrete political form. The State is always *in fieri*. It is all always in our hands. It is therefore our own immense responsibility.

But this State that realizes itself in the consciousness and will of the individual, rather than being imposed from on high, cannot have the same relationship with the people imagined by Nationalism. They imagined that the State corresponded with the nation, and conceived both as an already existing entity that it was not necessary to create, but which it was only necessary to come to know. That preexisting entity required a ruling class, characteristically intellectual, that sensed that entity, that first required to be known, understood, appraised, and exalted. The authority of the State was not a product, but a presupposition. It could not depend on the people, in fact, the people depended on the State. The authority that the people were required to recognize was the very precondition of life. Without that authority, sooner or later, one would have to acknowledge that survival was not possible. The Nationalist state was aristocratic state, that constructed itself out of the force it inherited from its origin, that made it valued by the masses. The Fascist State, on the other hand, is a popular state, and, in that sense, a democratic State par excellence. The relationship between the State and the individual is not that between it and one or the other citizen, but with every citizen. Every citizen shares a relationship with the State that is so intimate that the State exists only in so far as it is made to exist by the citizen. Thus, its formation is a product of the consciousness of each individual, and thus of the masses, in which the power of the State consists. That explains the necessity of the Fascist Party and of all the institutions of propaganda and education that foster the political and moral ideals of Fascism, so that the thought and the will of the solitary person, the Duce, becomes the thought and the will of the masses. Out of that arises the enormous difficulty in which it is involved, to bring into the Party, and into the institutions created by the Party, all the people—commencing from their most tender years. It is a formidable problem, the solution of which creates infinite difficulty, because it is almost impossible to conform the masses to the demands of an elite Party of vanguard morality. Such a conformity could only happen slowly, through education and reform. Equally difficult is the duality between governmental action and the action of the Party. As the Party's organization expands almost to the full extent of the State—whatever the effort to consolidate their efforts through the force and unity of discipline, discrepancies remain. The two, however much the effort is made to make their action one through discipline, the danger remained that there would be difficulty, with every initiative and progress—given that all individuals were bound together in a mechanism that, even though encouraged by a single spirit that emanated from the center and proceeded to the periphery, the freedom of movement and autonomy would only slowly languish and disappear.

XIV. The Corporative State

The great social and constitutional reform that Fascism is accomplishing, instituting the corporative syndicalist regime as a substitute for the liberal State, arose out of the very character of the Fascist State. Fascism accepted from Syndicalism the idea of the educative and moral function of the syndicate. But since the intention was to overcome the antithesis between the State and the syndicate, the effort was made to enter the system of syndicates harmoniously into corporations subject to discipline by the State and to thereby give expression to the organic character of the State. In order to give expression to the will of the individual, the organic State must reach him, not as an abstract political individual that the old liberalism supposed—as a featureless atom. The organic State sought to reach the individual as it could only find him, as he in fact is: as a specialized producer whose tasks moved him to associate himself with others of the same category, all belonging to the same unitary economic organism that is the nation. The syndicate, conforming as much as possible to the concrete reality of the individual, renders him valued for what he is in reality—be it in terms of self-consciousness that he gradually achieves, or from the right he has earned as a consequence of a contribution, through the syndicate, to the general interests of the nation.

This major reform remains in process. Nationalism and syndicalism—together with liberalism, itself—had criticized the old representative form of the liberal State and appealed to a system of organic representation to better capture the reality in which citizens are lodged, and would better represent their psychology and provide support for the development of their personality.

The corporative State seeks to approximate itself to the notion of immanence of the State in the individual. That immanence provides for both the strength of the State [because it is identified with the individual] and the liberty of the individual [because the liberty of the individual is found in the liberty of the State]. That concept provides [the rationale] for the ethical and religious values that Fascism has made its own and which the Duce has regularly invoked in his speeches...in the most solemn manner.

XV. Liberty, Ethics and Religion

On one occasion the Duce of Fascism undertook a discussion of the theme: *Force or Consensus?* concluding that the two terms are inseparable—that the one entails the other—the one incapable of being affirmed without the affirmation of the other. That implies that the authority of the State and the liberty of citizens is an infrangible circle in which authority presupposes liberty and vice versa. Liberty is found only in the State and the State is authority. The State is not an abstraction, an entity that descends from heaven and remains suspended in air above the heads of citizens. Rather, it is all one with the personality of the individual, who for that reason must foster, seek out, and recognize the State, knowing that it is that which he has, himself, fashioned.

Fascism, in truth, does not oppose itself to liberalism as a system of authority against a system of liberty. [It sees itself] rather as a system of true and concrete liberty as opposed to abstract and false liberty. Liberalism commences with the breaking of the circle above indicated—opposing the individual to the State, and liberty to authority. Liberalism seeks a liberty in itself, that confronts the State. It wants a liberty that is the limit of the State, resigning itself to a belief that the State is the (unfortunately inevitable) limit of liberty. These were abstractions and inanities that were the object of criticism within liberalism itself by those liberals of the nineteenth century who valued and anticipated the necessity of a strong State—in the interests of liberty. The merit of Fascism was that it courageously and vigorously opposed itself to the prejudices of contemporary liberalism—to affirm that the liberty proposed by liberalism serves neither the people nor the individual. Moreover, since the corporative State tends to realize, in the most coherent and substantial manner, the unity and comprehensiveness of authority and liberty through a system of representation more genuine and more in correspondence with reality, the new State is more liberal than the old.

Within that circle [of authority and liberty]—unrealizable except in the sphere of individual consciousness which historically developed in association with the productive forces and in the historic tradition of intellectual and moral conquests—the State could not attain the concreteness to which it aspires and of which it has need, if it did not invest in that sphere all its consciousness as a sovereign force not circumscribed by any limit or condition. Otherwise, the State, in the very intimacy of its spirit, would remain suspended in air. Only that is valuable, and lives, that is entirely spirit—omitting nothing. The authority of the State is not subject to negotiation, or compromise, or to divide its terrain with other moral or religious principles that might interfere in consciousness. The authority of the State has force and is true authority if, within consciousness, it is entirely unconditioned. The consciousness that actuates the reality of the State is consciousness in its totality, with all the elements of which it is the product. Morality and religion, essential elements in every consciousness, must be there, but they must be subordinated to the laws of the State, fused in it, absorbed in it. The human being, who in the profundity of his will, is the will of the State with its synthesis of the two terms of authority and liberty—each acting on the other to determine its development—is the human being who, through that will, slowly solves religious and moral problems. The State, without these determinations and these values, would devolve into a mechanical thing. It would be divested of that value to which it politically pretends. *Aut Caesar, aut nihil.*

Out of this arises the exquisitely political character of the relationships between the Fascist State and the Roman Catholic Church. The Italian Fascist State—for reasons already given—one with the mass of Italians, is either not religious, or it is Roman Catholic. It cannot be irreligious, because the absolute value and authority it confers on itself would be incomprehensible without a relationship to a divine Absolute. It would be a religion that had a base, was rooted in, and made sense to, the mass of the people of Italy. That would allow the absolute will of the Fatherland, of which there could only be one, to find expression in a religious sentiment. The alternative would be to stupidly fail to develop that which was already in consciousness, or to arbitrarily introduce into consciousness that which it did not contain. To be a Catholic meant to live in the Church and under its discipline. Therefore, it was a necessity for the Fascist State to recognize the religious authority of the Church; a political necessity, a political recognition, with respect to the realization of the State itself. The ecclesiastical politics of the Italian State must resolve the problem of maintaining its sovereignty, intact and absolute, even before the Church, without casting itself athwart the Catholic consciousness of Italians, nor the Church to which that consciousness is subordinated.

That is a grave problem, since the transcendent conception that rules over the Catholic Church contradicts the immanentist character of the political conception of Fascism—which, as has been said, far from being the negation of liberalism and democracy (which even the leaders of Fascism have regularly repeated for polemical reasons) actually aspires to be the most perfect form of liberalism and democracy, in conformity with the doctrine of Mazzini, to whose spirit Fascism has returned.

This is the way. A long, harsh, steep way. The Italian people have commenced on the path with a faith, with a passion, that has taken possession of the soul of the crowd, and for which there are no examples in its history. They undertake passage with a discipline never before experienced, without hesitation, without discussion, with eyes only for that person of heroic temper, gifted with those extraordinary and admirable traits of the great leaders of peoples. That Leader advances, secure, surrounded in an aura of myth, almost a person chosen by the Deity, tireless and infallible, an instrument employed by Providence to create a new civilization.

Of that civilization one can divine that which has contingent value specific to Italy—and that which has permanent and universal value.

August 1927

Appendices

1. The Philosophy of Fascism*

Every political conception truly worthy of the name is a philosophy, because it is not possible to isolate its proper object—political life in general, the political life of a determinate people in a determinate time—from other forms of human reality, that ordinarily maintain themselves distinctly from politics. Nor can politics isolate itself from universal reality, historic or natural. It cannot be isolated because man with all his activity, when he is not abstractly considered, is intimately related to all reality. Only in such a relationship can the human being understand himself and find guidance. A self-sufficient politics could not serve. Politics invests everything, as does ethics, with which, in a certain fashion, it identifies itself.

Fascism has a full awareness of that truth—and therefore accentuates the ethical character of the conception that it proposes. And, in spite of the polemics against philosophy with which many Fascist writers content themselves, it does attribute a philosophical significance and a universal application to its affirmations as affirmations of principles—whose consequences are of interest not only to politics in the strict sense, but economy, law, science, art and religion itself—in fact, to every human activity, theoretical or practical.

The suspicion and aversion that many Fascists entertain with respect to philosophy are themselves indications and manifestations of the particular character of Fascist thought. As in many similar cases, they are the polemics of one philosophy against other philosophies. Fascism, in fact, polemicizes against abstract and intellectualistic philosophies (the rejection of intellectualism has become the common feature of Fascist literature)—that is to say, those philosophies that presume to explain life by putting themselves outside of it. The Fascist, on the other hand, conceives philosophy as a philosophy of practice (*praxis*). That concept was the product of certain Marxist and Sorellian inspirations (many Fascists and the Duce, himself, received their first intellectual education in the school

---

* An English language version of this article appeared as "The Philosophy of the Modern State," in the *Spectator*, 3 November 1928, pp. 36-37. The present article has been retranslated from the original.

of Marx and Sorel)—as well as the influence of contemporary Italian idealistic doctrines from which Fascist mentality drew substance and achieved maturity. Fascist philosophy is not a philosophy that is thought, it is rather one that is done. It therefore announces and affirms itself not with formulae, but with action. If it does make recourse to formulae, it attributes to them the same value as actions, in so far as they are expected to produce, not empty words, but practical effects.

From this fundamental character of Fascist philosophy derives those qualities that are spoken of as Fascist *style*—a style of literary expression and a style of practical conduct inspired by an economy and an austerity that would suppress in discourse, as it does in its treatment of facts, every superfluous element, tending to extract from human activity the maximum yield with respect to the superior ends toward which these activities should be directed. With that, the *form* of the Fascist conception defines itself. It is a form that has a determinate *content* which turns on the concept of the State—the center of its entire system of thought. The Fascist State may be defined in negative terms, affirming what it is not rather than what it is. That is so because the Fascist State has arisen as antithetical to the socialist and liberal conception. From that antithesis has arisen the energy with which Fascism has articulated its own conception of the State. It is understood that at the bottom of the anti-socialist and anti-liberal battle there was something positive—the ethical conception of the State as an autonomous personality that has its own value and its own ends, subordinating to itself every existence and individual interest, not to suffocate them, but to recognize them only as realizations of the personality of the State, as consciousness, and as will.

It is an anti-individualistic conception, in so far as it affirms a spiritual reality, a reality that is universal—not the result, but the ideal principle and the original source of the concrete life of individuals possessed of moral value. From that concept a form of the authoritarian State can be logically derived. It is an authoritarianism that is—only for those who do not know how to conceive ideas except in their abstraction—the negation of political liberty. Fascist authoritarianism rejects license—which is not liberty at all. Only through the State can liberty be realized, and therefore has never existed except as it manifests itself as the liberty of the State (not of the individual)—that is to say, the liberty of the State that realizes its existence in the better part of the consciousness and will of the citizen. That State is an effective existence. There is no question of being or not being concerning the State. The true State is not a State shaped by laws that are infirm and uncertain, prey to the perplexity and doubt that arises from individual judgment, but an institution animated by an unshakable superior and dominant will.

It is an authoritarian State that does not accept the anarchic liberalism of the individualist—who does not recognize the a priori and immanent necessity of the State. And yet, it is more liberal than the liberal State itself. The Fascist State, having organized and juridically recognized workers' syndicates and employer organizations, intends to adapt its structure to those united syndicates, to draw them into national corporations, on the way to a system of political representation compatible with the structure of workers' organizations—that is to say, to a system that adapts itself to the immediate concrete conditions of Italy's population, in which one finds the root of popular consciousness. It is a perfection of the representative system which the liberal State could not even imagine. But the national will of Fascism does not derive its political value from fact, but from the idea that informs and explains the history of a people's past and future. The ideal nation—that in the very awareness of its being, incarnates and reveals itself in, and to, few individuals or in a single individual—is more real than the factual nation that might exist, at any given time, in the awareness of ignorant and unknowing multitudes.

The Fascist conception is idealistic and appeals to faith, and celebrates ideal values (family, Fatherland, civilization and the human spirit) as superior to every contingent value. And it proclaims a morality of sacrifice and militancy, in response to which the individual must always be ready to face even death for a reality superior to himself. As a result, Fascism has been moved by its own logic to awaken the religious consciousness of Italians—and seeks to provide for the education of youth in schools and in premilitary institutions, founded and organized in a system that commences in earliest childhood until induction into the military.

1928

2. The Laws of the Grand Council*

Editor's Note: Gentile's discussion of the law regularizing the constitutional role of the Grand Council of Fascism is instructive in so far as he therein signals the transformation of the liberal, parliamentary, into the totalitarian, single party, state. The Grand Council was a council composed of the leaders of the Fascist revolution and, as such, was extra-constitutional from its inception. While composed exclusively of Fascist party leaders, the Grand Council spoke for the entire nation, controlling the initiation and the promulgation of legislation. Until 1928, in effect, the functions of the Grand Council were extra-legal. In that year, the law of the Grand Council to which Gentile refers, rendered the Council's activities lawful. More than that, the law of the Grand Council, for all intents and purposes, made the Head of the Government, Mussolini, and the members of the Council, the final arbiters of what was to count as constitutional law for the nation. After the passage of the law of the Grand Council, not a vestige of the liberal parliamentary system remained. It is in that context that Gentile's comments are instructive.

It is impossible to allow the law of the Grand Council to pass without a few words of comment, since it has given rise to thousands of expositions and judgments by journalists of the entire world, and concerning which one might imagine that everything had been said. Its importance is such that everything that has been said is nothing compared to that with which history will concern itself. A constitutional law of this kind is the beginning of a new history, to which the journals allude. But it has not been from this point of view, in general, that the law has been considered.

There are two ways to consider and appraise a law: juridical and political. The second easily transforms itself into the first— since whoever speaks of the political significance of a law frequently closes with a consideration that is entirely juridical, from which the political spirit remains extrinsic.

The jurist considers the form of the law, its coherence, its relationship to the system of State laws. When one deals, as in the present case, with constitutional law, all the interests of the jurist concentrates itself on the examination of the compatibility or incompatibility of the new laws and the fundamental Statute.[18]

---

* Published in *Educazione fascista*, September 1928.

The political, on the other hand, looks toward the substance of the law—any law—which never limits itself exclusively to its technical content (finance, public health, economy, education, etc.), but conforms to the political reality to whose development all laws, more or less, contribute.

But true political considerations would not limit themselves, as is often the case, to the study of the relationship between political tendencies already defined, laws extant in legislative and institutional forms, and the new laws introduced into the juridical system of the State. In doing so, one returns from the political point of view to the juridical. The judgments tendered take on a formal and theoretical character, one might say retrospective character—for they define past as well as present reality. They are reflections on that reality. They do not simply accept past development, but rather commit themselves to the formation of a new consciousness—in whose realization consists the entire political life of a people—its evolving history. One does not undertake politics, or make history solely by promulgating new laws, creating new institutions, or winning battles, but also (and properly) by developing new spiritual attitudes, new ideas, and creating, in fact, new human beings and a new spirit.

Political considerations are not theoretical, but practical, in the most exquisite sense of the word. They look not to the past, but to the future. They are not animated by intellectualistic interests, conceptual or formal systematizations, but by a profound sense of the historic reality of the nation and its development. They therefore consider the real nucleus, the historically significant and actual substance of laws. Political considerations are never extraneous to the political form in which the process of national life, in its unity, finds expression.

Perhaps this has been too long a preamble—but it is not pointless in the present circumstances, considering that it might be of assistance to persons in recognizing the new political situation in which Italy finds itself since the 20th of September 1928. After that date, it was no longer appropriate to appeal to the categories of political judgments which had hitherto served in the daily polemics between Fascists and anti-Fascists about the Fascist revolution, and on which turned the contrast of the two terms equally vital and operative: Constitution and Revolution. It was a contrast which the Fascist regime sought to gradually resolve by constitutionalizing the Revolution. There arose at every step the opposition of the paladins of the

Constitution—directed against the representatives of the Revolution. Conversely, the followers of the Revolution were provoked to attack the institutions and the authority of the State organized in accordance with the old Constitutional norms. The last typical example of that contrast arose in the Senate around the electoral law—at which time the Head of the Government had reason to affirm, in concluding the debate, that Fascists and their adversaries spoke two different languages. They were different languages because the adversaries of Fascism raised a simple legal question (that involved above all the constitutional form of the Fascist Grand Council that was very active politically) while Fascists were occupied with singularly political issues.

Today, every equivocation has been eliminated. The Constitution has been fundamentally altered. The formal basis for any discussion by the constitutional jurists of the opposition has been removed. The liberals of one time who were the defenders of the Constitution and the State—in so far as the latter had its structure and its guarantee in the Constitution, and who presented themselves as the guardians of order—have now either abandoned the field or have assumed a posture diametrically opposed to the one previously held. This is true because the liberty they sought was never an abstract and anarchical individualistic liberty—it was the liberty of the individual within the State and within the fundamental laws of the State. That liberty, by virtue of the laws of the Grand Council, is now Fascist liberty, that is to say, the liberty of the citizen whose will is explicated and actuated through a new system of constitutional life. In that life, among other things, representation is no longer bicameral but tricameral. The third representative house, which concentrates and purifies every element of the national will that is singularly political, brings together and organizes every effective force that pretends to represent and interpret that will. That third house of representation, in accordance with the classical principle of every State constitution, shares power with the Monarchy. It is a power that is truly the result, and at the same time, the principle of State personality in which the national tradition and conservative interests reconcile themselves to the dynamism of popular life in its historic development.

The two major articles of the law are those that assign to the Grand Council the formation of the list of Deputies nominated to parliament, to be then subject to election by the nation.[19] That is coupled with the preparation of a list of counsellors from which the Crown might select the Head of Government.

The first article does not destroy, but establishes the popular and progressive character of national representation; and the second does not deny the King, as is proper in a monarchical State, the selection of a Head of Government with the assistance of his ministers—just as it was in the parliamentary system when the selection involved the advice of parliament. In fact, the new system reinforces the prerogatives of the Crown. If the fluctuating majority in parliament was, in fact, free of every limitation, directive, and corrective action of the Crown, in the new Fascist regime the constitution of the Grand Council is anything but the result of a *contingent* national will. All of its ordinary members receive the approval of the King. They are drawn from the hierarchical organization of all the spontaneous forces of national life. It is true that [in pre-Fascist times] parliamentary recommendations [to the King] was a practice and not specifically a constitutional right. Precisely for that reason it had an elasticity and an indeterminate character that, as we can observe in the experiment with proportionality, succeeded in entirely nullifying, in practice, the discretionary power in choice exercised by the Crown. Choice, in the old parliamentary system, became subject to the arbitrary play [of majorities produced by] various combinations of groups, including mercurial little groups. The new written law and the consequent discipline of the large numbers involved, compatible with the ulterior selection of the Sovereign, guarantees the compatibility of the national will with the supreme directive will of the Monarch. It provides a guarantee that tumult and lack of continuity will not disrupt the normal historical development of national life. [The new system provides for] liberty and order, progress as well as conservation of those vital and essential elements of the national organism—which are necessary, as is the case in every organism, if it is to develop. An organism cannot develop if it does not conserve and defend, unchanged and unchangeable, its fundamental nucleus and its living individuality.

The Fascist State possesses an acute awareness of its proper individuality—and, as a consequence, an equally solid and profound instinctive sense of its own conservation, together with a sense of its own power of development. It possesses a powerful concept of the absolute autonomy of its proper ethical personality and of the consequent continuity of its very being. All of which means that the

Fascist State opposes itself to every conception that would make it the result of contingencies. It conceives itself as the necessary principle and the origin of every value it acknowledges. In the Grand Council, as the vehicle of all those forces operating to sustain that State, it has fashioned an organ compatible with the Constitution. The Grand Council was initially created through the obscure instinct of great revolutionary forces. Through the Grand Council, the will of an extraordinarily gifted human being becomes an organic and enduring institution. That which appeared as an ordinary and contingent creation of an individual, becomes the constitutional structure of the nation. The hero depersonalizes himself and transforms himself into the spirit of his people—a spirit that organizes and disciplines all the energies necessary to sustain the new vital impulse from whence comes redemption—which has acquired consciousness of itself and of its proper destiny.

With the law of the Grand Council the Fascist Revolution completes its transformation and completely resolves itself in the State. The Party ceases to be a party among many. It sends its Secretary to the Council of Ministers. [The Party is no longer only a part of the forces that make up the governance of the nation.] As the organization of the great majority of the nation—or of the politically significant masses of the Italian people—the Party becomes the nation. Having brought forth the government out of itself, the government is recognized by the people and the people are governed by it. The minorities that remain at the margins of national life are, by the Party, through the Grand Council, made valuable insofar as they can make a moral contribution to that life. They are means or instruments, rather than the subjects of the political life of the nation. Political life truly coincides with the Party, insofar as it adheres to the Regime—or rather, to the spirit which informs and sustains the life of the nation. The Party is totalitarian in law and in fact—because politically, law prevails over fact and not vice versa.

With the constitutionalization of the Fascist Regime the new history begins in which all Italians are invited to collaborate under the emblem of the Lictor's Rods—no longer to be Fascists and anti-Fascists, but Italians—no longer revolutionaries or defenders of the old regime, but citizens of the new Italy, united in the common proposition that they all take part in the grandeur and power of the nation. Within the State there is liberty with discipline; outside the State there is nothing. Within the new laws every right is sacred, because every right is a duty. It is a duty of the citizen to himself, because it is a duty to the Fatherland.

It is a new ideal, to which the Fascist Party is and must be responsible. The Fascist Party, in its triumph, feels the enormous weight of the responsibility it has assumed.

1928

Notes

1. Over the years the Italian parliament, through custom, had become responsible for the declaration of war. On the occasion of the declaration of war in 1915, the king had restored that power to himself.
2. See Giuseppe Mazzini, *The Duties of Man and Other Essays* (London: J. M. Dent, 1912) and Bolton King, *The Life of Mazzini* (London: J. M. Dent, 1914).
3. See Gentile's treatment of the thought of the Risorgimento, with its emphasis on that of Giuseppe Mazzini. Gentile, *Albori della nuova Italia: Varietà e documenti* (Lanciano: Carabba, 1923), Parts 1 and 2.
4. See Gentile, *Rosmini e Gioberti: Saggio storico sulla filosofia italiana del Risorgimento* (Florence: Sansoni, 1958).
5. See the entire discussion in Gentile, *Le origini della filosofia contemporanea in Italia* (Messina: Giuseppe Principato, 1917) in three parts.
6. Gentile always capitalized the term "State." That practice will be followed throughout the translations.
7. See the account of the period provided by Alfredo Oriani, *La lotta politica in Italia* (Rocca San Casciano: Cappelli, 1956), Books 8 and 9. Gentile approved of Oriani's account. See Mussolini's assessment of Oriani's work in his "Preface" to Alfredo Oriani, *La rivolta ideale* (Bologna: Cappelli, 1943), pp. iii-v.
8. Gentile's reform of education in 1923 restored religious education to the elementary schools in Italy.
9. Under the Fascist regime, Masonry was to be suppressed; see Alfredo Rocco, "Le leggi di difesa," *La trasformazione dello stato: Dallo stato liberale allo stato fascista* (Rome: "La Voce," 1927), pp. 35-58.
10. See Giuseppe Mazzini, "To the Italian Working Class" and "To The Italians," *The Duties of Man and Other Essays*, pp. 1-3, 221-247.
11. See the account of Ardigò, one of the principal positivists of the period, Giovanni Marchesini, *Roberto Ardigò: L'uomo e l'umanista* (Florence: Felice le Monnier, 1922).
12. See Gentile, *Studi vichiani* (Florence: Felice le Monnier, 1927).
13. See Gentile, *Il modernismo e i rapporti fra religione e filosofia* (Florence: Sansoni, 1962).
14. In this context see the exposition of Curzio Malaparte when he wrote as "the most formidable pen of Fascism," in Curzio Malaparte, "L'Europa vivente," in *L'Europa vivente e altri saggi politici (1921-1931)* (Florence: Vallecchi, 1961). In terms of the Fascist conception of revolutionary violence, see the exposition in Sergio Panunzio, *Diritto, forza e violenza: Lineamenti di una teoria della violenza* (Bologna: Cappelli, 1921); for a discursive account of Panunzio's views, see A. James Gregor, "Some Thoughts on State and Rebel Terror," in David C. Rapoport and Yonah Alexander (eds.), *The Rationalization of Terrorism* (Frederick, MD.: Aletheia

Books, 1982), pp. 56-66. For comparative purposes, see Leon Trotsky, *Terrorism and Communism* (Ann Arbor: University of Michigan, 1961).
15. This was one form of the armed political party that characterizes one category of revolutionary parties. The Nazi SS was another form. The Red Army, and the People's Liberation Army, still others.
16. In this context, see Gentile, "Mazzini e la Nuova Italia," "Risorgimento e fascismo," and "Il pensiero italiano del secolo XIX," in *Memorie italiane e problemi della filosofia e della vita* (Florence: Sansoni, 1936), pp. 23-42, 115-120, 221-244.
17. In this context, see Gentile, *Manzoni and Leopardi: Saggi critici* (Milan: Treves, 1928).
18. At the time of the revisions of the Statuto of 1848 by which Italy was governed until the Fascist reforms, constitutional reform could be conducted "piecemeal" by means of ordinary legislation. The *Statuto* contained 84 brief articles that were simply broad declarations of principle. As the *Statuto* matured through practice, there was no Italian court charged with the responsibility of passing on the constitutionality of acts adopted by parliament or promulgated by the monarch. Once Mussolini received, from the Italian parliament, the power to decree legislation, he could transform the *Statuto* by integrating and adjusting legislation to meet the ends of Fascism. In 1928, Mussolini had Italian law take cognizance of a distinction between "ordinary" and "constitutional" legislation when the Fascist Grand Council was made a major agency of the State, and afforded the power of passing on all "questions having a constitutional character." The Grand Council, chosen by Mussolini (and confirmed by the King), thus became a central organ of the State.
19. The similarities with the system that had emerged in Stalin's Soviet Union require no comment.

Selections from *What is Fascism?*

The Two Italys (pp. 13-16)

To begin with, you are asked to consider if it is not the case that the two distinct and different images of the Italy we have identified do not emerge from history. In truth, we all seek Italy. History is not a past that is of interest only to the erudite—it is present, alive, in the soul of us all. Those who are Italians feel themselves a part of this Italy. They find themselves not only in the blue of its sky, in its hills and its water, nor only in the desolate or mountainous land that alternates with its fruitful plains and its smiling gardens. We close our eyes, let us make abstraction from the horizons of its landscapes so varied in beauty and light—and Italy remains in our soul; in fact, it enlarges and expands in the glory of that which it is. In the mind and the heart of all civilized human beings who appreciate it, or at least recognize it, Italy is recognized as a nation of intelligence, and of a millennial culture that has never been eclipsed, of art and of solitary thinkers, of tormented civil life because of internal difficulty, of a national society slow in its labored process of organization and unification amidst foreign powers struggling in the vast organizing process of modern Europe. All, observing this more or less, and more or less involved, cognizant and sensing, have been, in themselves, unable to separate themselves from this historic living Italy, with a life that has roots buried deep in the centuries. It remains Italy, with its national characteristics—characteristics that became increasingly more evident...as the communes grew out of the defeated Empire, with liberty and art as their driving impetus. Italy was preparing for the Renaissance. The Renaissance was the most creative product of the Italian spirit, the most splendid beacon for everyone everywhere, which doubly inspired the Italians to seek access to the new science, new art, new thought, new faith—in ef-

---

* Giovanni Gentile, *Che cosa è il fascismo: Discorsi e polemiche* (Florence: Vallecchi, 1925).

fect—to the modern age. That Italy that we all carry in our hearts, and which forms, in fact, the substance of our being and of our character—if we watch it intensely today, with a gaze made more acute by our desire for a more elevated and powerful national life, with a passion that we cherish within ourselves after the agony of defeat and the pride of victory in the Great War—that Italy presents itself to us in two manifestly different forms. We see two Italys before us—one old and the other new.

There is the Italy of the ages, which is our glory but which is also our sad legacy, heavy on our shoulders and a burden to our spirits. It is a legacy which we must candidly admit is a disgrace of which we would be free—for which we must make amends. That great Italy of the ages, that has so large a place in the history of the world, that is recognized and studied and investigated by all civilized people, is the Italy whose history is not a particular history, but an epoch in universal history: the Renaissance.

In the Renaissance there is much light, yes, and there is much in it with which Italians may share national pride. But there is much darkness. For the Renaissance is also the age of individualism, that through the splendid visions of poetry and art brought the Italian nation to the indifference, skepticism, and distracted cynicism of those who have nothing to defend, not in their family, their Fatherland, or in the world where every human personality conscious of its own value and personal dignity invests itself. The Italians of the period had nothing to defend because they did not believe in anything beyond the free and pleasurable play of their own creative fantasy. From thence, came the frivolity of a pattern of behavior both decadent and corrupt. That behavior slowly extinguished the active sentiment of nationality and thereby enfeebled souls. The literature that arose was one in which carnival songs and bizarre burlesque of every sort were combined in a comedy that drew from the mockery of storytellers, witty and cynical, its material and its spirit—a comedy that is, however, never true art, which has one sense—the pain beneath the laughter....It is an empty literature, superficial, without soul. Sonnets, songs in abundance—but never a person who expresses his passion in song. Cultural institutions appear uncertain. As much culture as one wishes, but sterile, dead. Persons without will, without character, life without purpose. [All of that is the culture] of particular individuals who think of themselves and nothing more. An Italy of strangers, not of Italians. Italians without faith and therefore absent. Is not this the old, decadent Italy?

The Residues of the Old Italy (pp. 16-17)

That Italy, for us, is dead. Thankfully, there is another. It can be said, in a certain sense, that the old Italy has been dead for two centuries. But not so dead that we do not find it, at times, before us even today, in this year of grace 1925. There remain too many people in Italy who do not believe in anything and ridicule everything, sighing for the tranquility of the schools and academies—taking umbrage with those who disturb their digestion. Do you recall the eve of the Great War when the few believers dragged off the many who shrugged their shoulders repeating that old canard of foreigners that Italians were incapable of committing themselves—when our youth felt the thrill of an obscure instinct and gave themselves over entirely to the nation, blindly confidant in its fate, in the power of the people, in the necessity of a great and horrible test that would solidify the nation's recent unification—before that time more conceived in mind than believed in. The fiber of Italians had not been tested, realized, and tempered in battle—a battle for which every free people must always be ready. The mature men, the wise ones, smiled and calculated, and were horrified by the thought, as they would say, of futile sacrifices. They trembled at those dangers that, because of prudence, had never been confronted and would never be confronted by anyone not animated by an indemonstrable faith. Today that cowardly, myopic, and skeptical neutralism is synonymous, for many Italians, with an inability to deal with Italian problems as Italians. But that kind of spiritual temperament is of the old style. It undertakes no effort because of a lack of belief; it flees from courage because no advantage is recognized in the sacrifice, measuring national fortunes only in terms of individual well being, preferring always to travel where the way is solid, never to compromise oneself, never to become involved, leaving ideals to poets, to women, and particularly to philosophers, setting aside every question that might jeopardize the settled and quiet life, and is content making jest of everything and anything, always seeking to deflate any poetic enthusiasm, recommending moderation at all costs, and exhibiting a sacred horror of polemics and violence, making its own all the maxims of egoism—reflecting, studying, and understanding them as though they were the quintessence of cleverness and wisdom. Is not all of this, for many, the *non plus ultra* of the shrewdness peculiar to Italians?

There are the Masons who, it is acknowledged, have driven their secular principles to logical conclusion: they are neither for religion nor against it. That is the case not only for Masons, but for how many Italians who prefer to be silent on religious matters, have reservations, and are ashamed of revealing and defending their own convictions—if they have any.

All of this is the old Italy, the Italy of individualism, the Italy of the Renaissance—when even the sacrifice of philosophers was sterile because not honored, and not honored because it conformed to the logic of their own doctrines, all individualistically closed up in a world without connections to that life in which was to be found that concrete reality with which they necessarily had to deal and for which they were necessarily required to sacrifice. Human beings did not feel that their personality was an intrinsic part of the social world to which each belonged, in which each lived his own interests, with his family, with his faith as a moral person that has duties, with a program to realize and a truth to profess. There is nothing alive in the recesses of our soul that does not wish expression, to preach that which is our truth, to communicate it to all, to strengthen it with all the energy that derives from collaboration, from living together, from rendering common our moral life. Every faith draws persons together...

Mazzini (pp. 23-24)

Even in the times of Mazzini, there were liberals who gave the individual priority before all else. We still have those liberals underfoot who prove recalcitrant, and resist the irresistible movement of history. Liberalism, during the time of Mazzini, raised a fiery banner, the flag of liberty—that banner of liberty that even Mazzini adored and for which he struggled. Liberty at that time, politically, was necessary for the nation in its struggle against foreigners and was necessary for the citizens in their struggle against the State. It was thus, a matter of principle. But Mazzini maintained that true liberty was not that of individualistic liberals who failed to recognize the nation as superior to the individual, and did not thereby acknowledge the mission that awaited peoples, nor the sacrifice to which individuals are bound. Against that liberalism, Mazzini directed the charge of execrated, blind, and absurd materialism.

The Concept of the Nation (pp. 26-28)

Today we also affirm liberty—but within the State. The State is the nation, that nation that appears as something that limits us and subordinates us, and makes us sense and think and speak, and more than anything else, to *be* in a certain manner—Italians in Italy, children of our parents and of our history. All that is a fable, in the same fashion that nature, in general, with its laws is understood to have fashioned us in a certain form and figure, destined for a certain well-defined and immutable life is a fable. It all appears that way, but it is otherwise.

One of the major articles of the Mazzinian faith is the following: the nation is not a natural existence, but a moral reality. No one finds the nation at birth, everyone must work to create it. A people is a nation not in the sense that it has a history, an empirically established past, but only insofar as it feels its history, senses that history, and accepts it in living consciousness as its personality, that personality on which it is necessary to work day by day. As a consequence, it is a personality that one can never claim as a possession. It is not something that exists in nature—as might the sun, the hills, or the sea—personality is rather a product of an active will that constantly directs itself toward its ideal and which can thereby be said to be free. A people is a nation if it conquers its liberty, assessing its value and confronting all the pain that might be required in the course of that conquest, uniting its scattered members in a single body, redeeming them and founding an autonomous State, which is not a given, but a creation, with the assistance of the Deity, that is revealed and works in its own consciousness. This is the high Mazzinian conception of the nation, that can, in fact, reawaken national sentiment among Italians, posing our problem as a problem of education and revolution—a revolution without which not even Cavour was capable of making Italy. That is the nation—a nation through which Italians can only feel themselves forever connected with Mazzini's Young Italy and to those who today call themselves Fascists. The nation, in truth, is neither geography nor is it history: it is a program, a mission. And therefore, it is sacrifice. It is not, and will never be, a labor that is finished. It will never be that grand museum that Italy was at one time for Italians, who were its custodians, and in whose hands foreigners would leave a pittance when they came to visit. Yes, museums, galleries, monuments of an ancient grandeur and splendor will remain—not so that we might catch butterflies under the arch of Titus or mindlessly sit through academic commemorations in the Campidoglio, but rather to defend the memories with works that recapture the most ancient traditions and ennoble them in the present and the future. The memories are a patrimony to be defended not with erudition, but with new labor, and with all the arts of peace and war, which conserve that patrimony, renewing and increasing it. To the monuments, should they be chosen, new ones can be added. We should raise monuments in our plazas to reinforce our moral strength, to honor the living more than the dead. Monuments should be employed in consecrating more recent memory. Our recent past is really more glorious than that of history. Through the admonitions that emerge from generous recall, we should elevate our consciousness as free citizens of a great nation. Where the nation is conceived in such fashion, even liberty is more a duty than a right—another conquest obtained through the abnegation of the citizen prepared to give everything to the Fatherland without asking anything from it.

Fascism's Return to the Spirit of the Risorgimento (pp. 28-29)

This concept of the nation upon which we insist, is not an invention of Fascism. It is the soul of that Italy that slowly supercedes the old. Fascism is that vigorous sentiment of nationality that carried Italians into the fire of the Great War. Its impetus made it possible for them to prevail in that tragic test. It made energetic reaction to the materialism of yesterday that attempted to cancel the value of that test, and prostrate the spirit of Italians. There was a desperate discouragement—a weariness and desire for well being, the more impatiently coveted because more difficult to obtain. Fascism emphasized the grandeur and the beauty of the sacrifice endured as Italy's most significant legacy for the future. In doing so, Fascism once again powerfully shocked Italians in order to have them remember that they were the children of Italy—to bring once more to mind that which, beginning with the Risorgimento, made that Italy possible. Fascism sought to have Italians remember that which rendered our fathers ashamed of their servitude, to have them shake off inertia, to liberate themselves of the old rhetorical and literary remnants of the past and begin to speak seriously about liberty.

Fascism has returned to the spirit of the Risorgimento with that vigor that derived from the new consciousness that arose out of the Great War. The war was a test completed with honor by the Italian people. It provided a sense of a capacity to commit the nation, to win, and to count in the history of the world. It has returned with an impatience to awaken the nation from the recent and temporary confusion—the stupor that afflicted its consciousness—so that the product of its immense sacrifice in the Great War would not be lost. The fact is that Italy has earned a place as a great power—and that has almost been attained. That it has become a nation with its own will, must not be lost sight of. It should become the object of that will, to be conquered and firmly retained.

Fascist Violence (pp. 29-32)

In its impetuous ardor, Fascism has employed violence when it believed violence necessary. At a certain point, the persons of old Italy pretended to be scandalized by that. At first, Fascist violence served their interests—when the State appeared on the verge of collapse and was no longer capable of guaranteeing public order— something that created some inconveniences even for those who might be disposed to allow the moral values of the war to be lost and trampled upon. They had continued to give lip service to the Mazzinian religion of the nation as long as the individual enjoyed security of life, labor, and thought—the "natural" liberties. In other words, [Fascist violence was overlooked] as long as every gentleman that thought about himself and his family was allowed to live comfortably after the privations and the demands of the war!

During that initial period even the truncheons of the Fascist action squads were considered a divine intervention. But as soon as the reordering of the State provided for the security of normal life, the cause that made Fascist violence necessary was forgotten —it is easy to forget all that when the threats are past. It was not enough that the Head of the Fascist Government announced that the truncheon was retired to the attic. The argument was that the State, the product of Fascism, would promote and defend its own ideals. It was not enough that the Fascist squads became a regular, though voluntary, militia of the State. It was not enough that Fascism no longer wished to be a force external to the State. The truncheon, in all its material brutality, was made the symbol of the spirit of Fascist violence. Every crime, every abuse of power, every arrogance, committed by delinquents who identified themselves as Fascist was employed to identify Fascism, itself, as immoral. What seemed to have been forgotten is that every party that pursues revolutionary purpose—counting hundreds of thousands of followers in its ranks—must necessarily find among them delinquents, exploiters, and the arrogant. They had insinuated themselves into the Fascist Party. They, unfortunately, were recognized, at the cost of the movement, too late. Fascism was stamped immoral—the wrath of God.

What followed was an appeal to Franciscan sweetness and charity to one's neighbor that had never been heard before in Italy. There appeared a kind of Quakerism in Italy that had never been observed before. Those who have recognized that a State which is not strong is not a State—have always employed the moral question in order to shake a strong government. I do not wish to insist on that point. Old Italy must have patience, and concerning the moral question, must await the verdict of history. Fascism cannot be confounded with those men who, here or there, today of tomorrow, might represent it. Fascism is an idea, a spiritual movement, that has its own intrinsic force, born of its own truth, and its own response to profound historical and national needs. What everyone notes today is this curious fact: Fascism's adversaries, knowing that Fascism is an idea, do not direct their objections to one or another Fascist, but toward all Fascists without distinction—or at least toward those who come forward to defend Fascism. Against them, from dawn to dusk, these preachers of Franciscan benevolence—they now call themselves Liberals—hurl ridicule, invective, fantastic accusations, defamation, and calumny—knowing them to be such. It is linguistic violence and a calculated cynicism that would bring shame to a brigand. None of Fascism's opponents maintain any scruple—not even the intellectuals and philosophers that are found swarming, for obvious reasons, among the anti-Fascists. To say to a gentleman: you are a beast, or an exploiter, or violent, or an agent of crime or an instigator of delinquency—to our innocent Liberals, that is not violence. Because it appears only in print, violence is not violence. So much for the word-magic of those most devoted to the defense of the freedom of the press.

Now, we say it clearly once again for all persons of good will. There is violence and there is violence. No one worthy of marching under Fascist guidons has ever confused the two. Those who are not worthy of remaining with us—are to be expelled when discovered. There is private violence, which is arbitrary, anarchic, and which undermines society.[1] If Fascism is not a word devoid of meaning—something that even its adversaries do not pretend—private violence finds no more determined, more genuine, more formidable an enemy than Fascism. There is another violence, willed by God and by all men who believe in God and in order—in support of laws that God certainly wishes to obtain in the world.

It is clear to all men of good will that there is a violence that refuses to accept the notion that there is some parity between the law and the delinquent. One of Europe's great thinkers noted that were the delinquent possessed of right reason, he would freely choose, accept or demand, that punishment that is his due. The will of the law ethically annuls the will of the criminal—and expresses itself in a form of sanctioned violence. Moralists, beginning with Jesus, made recourse to violence when they were firmly convinced that violence represented the law—the will of a superior or universal interest. In the Catholic Church this is true not only for Dominicans but for the followers of Saint Francis.

With the State, that has always been true. When the State was in crisis, it has always been revolutionaries who employ violence to establish a new State.[2] Is not Fascism a revolution? Its idea is certainly revolutionary. Those who would deny that are those who foolishly propose that the March on Rome that brought Fascism to power might have been accomplished through pacific, bloodless, means—and are daily employed in deploring and denouncing the bloody and uncompromising violence of Fascism.

The Recurrent Barbarisms of Giambattista Vico (pp. 32-33)

We have cited, among those memorable founders of the new Italy, the great Neapolitan philosopher Giambattista Vico. Those who oppose Fascism will perhaps smile when we suggest that the good Catholic philosopher of the *Scienza nuova* is to be found among its spiritual masters. I would have them consider the "heroic morality" that found expression among humankind at the time when the old deities were abandoned, and families, society, and the State were founded, in accordance with the designs of providence—with force and violence. I would have them reconsider Vico's doctrine of waves of recurrent barbarism that bring in their train that violence which reorders and uplifts degenerate States. Their uplift produces the very liberty of those nations. It renders them more civil—where reason, fully explicated—slowly produces a regime of absolute civil equality.

How often has Fascism been charged with barbarism by malevolent dullards? Let them consider the precise significance of that barbarism—of which we boast.[3] It is a barbarism made up of a lucid energy destructive of false and baleful idols, restorative of the health of the nation and the power of the State by reaffirming its sovereign rights—which are, in fact, its duties. Our barbarism disdains that sham intellectualistic culture that corrupts and falsifies, and which is inclined to, and indulgent toward, individualistic velleities and anarchistic egoisms—just as it distains false piety and hypocritical fraternity. It abjures that etiquette that weans one away from rude and healthy candor and accustoms one to reciprocal deception and intolerable tolerances. We seek to provoke in the Italian soul an inextinguishable thirst for knowledge that is the labor and reform of the interior of humankind and the acquisition of the moral and material means for a life always more elevated, always more productive, for the individual and for the nation—in fact, for humanity and the world. We seek the enhancement of the world. We seek the enhancement of the world because we live in it and with it. We will educate our children—those young people, filled with enthusiasm, who have collected around us—to feel that life is not pleasure, but duty. If one loves one's neighbor, one is counseled not to provide him with, or facilitate his obtaining, the quiet life. Rather one should assist and prepare him for labor, for sacrifice. That conviction best embodies the love of parents for their children. Parental love is not caresses and blandishments; parents should seek, with workmanlike effort, to instill an austere and prescient vigilance in children until each is prepared and capable of dealing with life's necessities, with the laws of the world, with duty.

The Fascist Doctrine of the State (pp. 33-34)

From our Mazzinian consciousness of the sanctity of the nation—which, in reality, manifests itself as the State—we draw the reasons for our customary glorification of the State. To the old style skeptics, glorification of the State is nothing more than a new piece of rhetoric. They observe us with a wink and a smile—somewhere between foolishness and cunning—to repeatedly whisper: worship of the State! It is the response to be expected from a form of liberalism that Mazzini characterized as individualistic and materialistic.

At this moment, a thought comes to mind. In 1882, a noble person was wont to say that he was also a liberal, but a liberal of a good sort, one of those who really believed in liberty and loved it. We find ourselves at this juncture, he would say, lamenting the disorder of parliamentarianism and the arrogance of the radicals against the State. He held that they had reduced the State to an instrument of their caprices and of the fickle pretensions of the crowd and of cliques.

We have come to this: In Italy we have even forgotten the very etymological origins of the term "State." The State, with respect at least to individual whimsy, must remain, must rule, as something firm, solid, and indestructible. Law and force: Law is that which makes itself respected and which does not capitulate every time it fails to please the individual or does not favor this or that special interest. If it would be that force, it must be domestically and externally powerful—capable of realizing its proper will. A rational or reasonable will, as is the case with every will that cannot remain at the stage of simple velleity, but must translate itself into action and success. It must be a will that cannot allow others to limit it. It is, therefore, a sovereign and absolute will. The legitimate will of citizens is that will that corresponds to the will of the State, that organizes itself and manifests itself by means of the State's central organs. With respect to its external or international relations—war, in the last instance—tests and guarantees the sovereignty of the single State within the system of history, in which all States compete. In war, the State demonstrates its power, which is to say, its proper autonomy.

The Ethical State (pp. 34-36)

Only that State that wishes to be, is in fact, a concrete will—all others can be considered wills only abstractly. [If one considers solitary individuals as possessed of concrete will, one would, by implication, imagine that such a will could function independent] of the indissoluble ties by which each is bound to society and breathes in, as though it were part of the atmosphere, language, custom, thought, interests, and aspirations.

[It is the State that possesses a concrete will and] must be considered a person. In order to will, it is necessary to have consciousness of that which one wills, of ends and of means. To have such a consciousness, it is necessary, first of all, to have an awareness of oneself, to distinguish oneself from others, to affirm oneself in one's proper independence as a center of conscious activity—in effect, to be a person.

Whoever says person, says moral activity. One speaks of an activity that wills that which it should will, in accordance with an ideal. The State is that national consciousness, and the will of that consciousness—and draws from that consciousness the ideal toward which it aims and toward which it directs all its activity. The State, therefore, is an ethical substance. Allow the philosophical terminology. The significance is transparent, if each of you will refer to your own consciousness and feel the sanctity of the Fatherland that commands with orders that are not subject to discussion—and must be obeyed—throughout life, without hesitation, and without exception. The State, for us, has an absolute moral value—as that moral substance whose function it is to render all other functions valuable. By coinciding with the State, all other functions attain absolute value.

Keep in mind: human life is sacred. Why? Because man is spirit and as such has absolute value. Things are instruments, human beings are ends. And still, the life of the citizen, when the laws of the Fatherland demand it, must be sacrificed. Without these evident truths that have been planted in the heart of all civilized humanity, there could be no social life, no human life.

An ethical State? Liberals will object. They fail to understand the concept—and level against it the most emphatic protests. Although they pretend preoccupation with the moral order, they call upon traditions, whose principles are the denial of every moral reality. They lapse into that materialism common to the century in which the doctrine of classical liberalism was formulated.

Liberals contend that morality is the attribute of empirical individuals—who alone can possess will—the only personality in the proper sense of the term. The State is nothing other than the external limit on the behavior of a free independent personality—to assure that the behavior of one does no injury to others. This negative and empty concept of the State is absolutely rejected by Fascism—not because Fascism presumes to impose the State upon the individual, but because according to the teachings of Mazzini, it is impossible to conceive individuals in atomistic abstraction, and then have the State somehow integrate them into an impossible synthesis. We believe that the State is the very personality of the individual divested of accidental differences, shorn of the abstract preoccupations of particular interests, no longer seen or evaluated in the general system in which such concerns find their reality and the possibility of their effective realization. It is personality returned and concentrated in the deepest part of consciousness—where the individual feels the general interest as his own, and wills therefore as might the general will. This profound consciousness which each of us realizes and must realize within himself as national consciousness in all its dynamism, its juridical form, and in its political activity, the very foundation of our own personality—that is the State. To conceive the State external to moral life is to deny the individual, himself, the substance of his morality.

The Fascist ethical State, it must be recognized, is no longer the agnostic State of the old liberalism. Its ethical form is spiritual; its personality is cognizant; its system is will. To speak of "system" is to speak of thought, program. It is to speak of the history of a people gathered in the living fire of an actual and active consciousness. It is to speak of that which it is and that which it can, and must, be. It is to speak of mission and purpose—in general and in particular, remote and proximate, mediate and immediate—in specifics. The State is the encompassing will of the nation—and therefore its all encompassing intelligence. It neglects nothing and excludes itself from nothing that involves the interests of the citizen—whether economic or moral. Nothing human is alien to it. The State is not a great facade, nor is it an empty building—it is mankind itself, the edifice constructed, inhabited, and sustained by the joy and pain of labor and all the life of the human spirit.

Against the Accusation of Statolatry (pp. 36-37)

Is this statolatry? It is the religion of the spirit that has not been cast into the abject blindness of materialism. It is the torch raised by the youth of Fascism to ignite a vast spiritual conflagration in this

Italy that has arisen to struggle for its own redemption. Redemption is impossible if the nation cannot rehabilitate its internal moral forces, if it does not accustom itself to conceive life in its entirety as religious, if it does not train its citizens in that simple readiness to serve the ideal, to work, to live and to die for the Fatherland—that Fatherland that occupies the foremost place in thought, venerated, sanctified. The nation cannot be redeemed if the military and the school that renders a people powerful is not cherished; if the labor that is the foundation of all national and private wealth, the ground of will and character, is not cherished.

Fascism and the Working Classes (pp. 37-38)

Fascism is the most intransigent opponent of the myths and lies of international socialism—the myths and lies of those without a Fatherland and without duties, of those who offend the sentiment of right, and therefore of the individual, in the name of an abstract and empty ideal of human brotherhood. Fascism does not conceive of the strong ethical State as a leaden cape that would suffocate every spontaneity in the nation—but as the supreme form of that conscious unity composed of all the forces of the nation in their successive development. Fascism cannot exclude the proletariat—that was introduced and exalted by socialism—from the political arena. The ethical State must grow out of that very reality that includes the proletariat and must, therefore, conform itself to it.[4] The State's force and power derives from its ability to incorporate within itself all the vital constituents of the nation.

For that reason, Fascism occupies itself today with the reorganization of the working masses on a national foundation in conformity with its moral conception of the State.[5] It separates the State from the conventional untruths of the old parliament of professional politicians. Fascism seeks a form of governance in which all the social, economic, and intellectual forces are organized in an order more durable and solid, yet more dynamic—so that the healthy and sincere political currents of the nation would flourish.

I will not enter into particulars which may well be corollaries of Fascist doctrine, but which are not Fascism. It is not the corollaries that provide historic significance to our movement. The importance is in the idea, in its animating spirit—that spirit against which, we are certain, no lesser force can prevail.

Fascism is Religion (pp. 38-39)

...Fascism is a party, a political doctrine. But Fascism—in so far as it is a party, a political doctrine—is before all else a total conception of life. That is its force...its great merit, and the secret of the prestige it exercises over all those who are not victims of the malign and interminable maunderings of certain newspapers. One cannot be a Fascist in politics and not a Fascist...in school, not a Fascist in one's family, not a Fascist in one's workplace. Just as the Catholic, if a Catholic, invests all of his life with his religious sentiment, and speaks and works, or remains still, thinks and meditates...as a Catholic. Similarly, the Fascist—whether he goes to parliament or remains in the local association, writes in the newspapers or reads them, provides for his own private life or converses with others, looks to the future or remembers his past and the past of his people—must always remind himself that he is a Fascist!

Thus is revealed that which truly can be said to be the defining trait of Fascism—to take life seriously. Life is labor, effort, sacrifice, and hard work—it is a life in which we well know that there is no pleasure. There is no time for pleasure. Before us there is always the ideal to be realized, an ideal that does not allow us rest. We cannot lose time. Even asleep, we are responsible for the talents that we have been given. We must make them develop, not for ourselves who are of no account, but for our country, for the Fatherland—for that Italy that fills our heart with its memories and with its aspirations, with its joys and with its travails—that Italy that reproves us for the centuries our fathers lost. We are now comforted by recent events in which Italian power has miraculously reemerged—when Italy, in its entirety, collected itself in one thought, in one sentiment, in one willingness to sacrifice. It was, in fact, the youth, the Young Italy of the Prophet Mazzini, who were ready, who gave themselves to sacrifice, and died for the Fatherland. They died for the ideal for which only human beings can live and which makes of life something serious. We think of these recent events in which are concentrated all the longings of our people, in which and from which all the hopes of our future arise. Those of us who are conscious of being Italian, of being Fascists, know that we cannot fail to see those six hundred thousand of our dead, [lost in the Great War], arise before us to admonish us that life must always be taken seriously, that there is no time to lose, that Italy must be made as great as they had envisioned it in their final vision—as great as Italy can, and will be, if we also sacrifice for her, every day, forever.

The March on Rome (pp. 123-125)

In the March on Rome the entire Italian ideal movement of the first twenty years of this century found its outlet—a reaction against the ideologies that in Italy were prevalent during the last five decades of the nineteenth century, and that took shape in the democratic, socialist (at least in the spurious form in which Marxism assumed in the Latin countries), positivist, illuministic, and pseudorationalist conceptions of life and the world. What were the elements of this reaction: idealist philosophy, that exposed and overcame the materialism that was at the core of all these doctrines; the revival of religious sentiment; the syndicalism of Sorel with its moral and mystic tendencies; the Great War of 1914-1918.

The war was the crucible, in which the spiritual forces were fused that were taking shape in the ferment of youthful spirits, in the course of passionate, philosophic, or religious, literary or social, discussions. They fused and formed themselves in a concrete spiritual life, that is always act, will—the creative power of new forms. The youth of Italy, who had suffered and been tormented, felt that the war, was a grand and fatal experiment for the Italian people. All of this was to find expression in the war—a kind of judgment of God, in which this people that had never fought such a war, was required to unite in a national war of life or death. It involved a kind of mysticism which the war itself could not explain without reference to those antecedents that obscurely matured within souls.

After the war, Fascism seemed to explode like a violent cry from the youth of Italy—and at its commencement, it represented the impetuousness and vehemence of youth. Its violence—which was illegal, and necessarily led to revolution—was a form of the new thought, that could no longer find expression in abstractions, but was rather the constructive activity of a new moral life. The new philosophy no longer acknowledged ideas which, as such, were not will and action—it was held that one could no longer distinguish between theory and practice. The new philosophy taught that the human being who really thinks, profoundly, sensing the truth of his thought, living it, can only turn upon reality and involve himself in the forging of that world in which the truth of his ideas might be actualized and demonstrated.

In that respect, Fascism is a spiritual posture of the highest moral value and of singular historical significance. It is for that reason that the world looks upon Italy with intense interest. Among some of them there is the concern that there very well may be a Fascist Italy! Fascism for Italy is the new force of its redemption—the force that will redeem her from the centuries-long, millenarian, servitude, that until yesterday oppressed her. That servitude (and who does not know it?) was for a long period political slavery with the national incapacity to form a State. It was always an interior servitude, the product of a false belief that conceived thought as something other than action and *saying* something was other than *doing* something. It involved the belief that one might celebrate the ideal with a cult of noble thought and beautiful speech—without involving oneself in sacrifice, tears and blood. Fascism—that genuine thing of which Italian youth has made a religion, for which they are prepared to die—is the greatest victory that Italians have achieved against their greatest enemy: empty rhetoric.

Fascism and Its Opponents (pp. 42-45, 47-48, 49-51, 56.)

...The socialism to which Fascism opposes itself is only one among many of the forms of the degeneration of democracy that typify modern political society. It represents only one of the forms against which Fascism has opposed itself. Nor can it be said that socialism, in its entirety, has been the target of the violence of Fascism. It is necessary to distinguish between socialism and socialism—in fact between idea and idea of the same socialist conception, in order to distinguish among them those that are inimical to Fascism. It is well known that Sorellian syndicalism, out of which the thought and the political method of Fascism emerged—conceived itself the genuine interpretation of Marxist communism. The dynamic conception of history, in which force as violence functions as an essential, is of unquestioned Marxist origin. Those notions flowed into other currents of contemporary thought, that have themselves, via alternative routes, arrived at a vindication of that form of State—implacable, but absolutely rational—that finds historic necessity in the very spiritual dynamism through which it realizes itself.

Fascism combats the abstract class conception of society, rejecting the entire notion of antithetical class interests upon which the artificialities of "class struggle" rests. The concept has already been largely abandoned by theorists. Marxism succumbed to that criticism as quickly as it previously had been elevated by theorists. To the theoretical criticism, practical failure has been added with the advent of the Great War. In the circumstances of the Great War, individual societies were compelled to abandon all ideologies—in order to adapt themselves to reality. They were forced to do so by the internal and irresistible logic of their own organic nature. [The very needs of the war] testified to the solidarity and intimate unity, both moral and economic, of the constitutive classes of the social and State organism.

With apostolic vigor, Fascists opposed in Marxism the same thing that Mazzini had opposed. Mazzini was the prophet of our Risorgimento and, as a consequence of many features of his doctrine, the master of today's Fascism. Both Mazzinianism and Fascism reject the utilitarian, materialistic, and egoistic conception of life—seeing life as an arena for the discharge of duties, with sacrifice of oneself in the service of an ideal. The Marxism that Fascism opposes restricts the breadth of our thought and of the human heart, representing history as a grand theater of economic interests. Fascism confronts it with the same method as that of Giuseppe Mazzini: not with abstract theoretical argument, but with action, which it actuates and inculcates in youthful hearts.

More than that, Marxism has emerged as an anti-national and subversive adversary of the Fascist Party. It is only one of Fascism's adversaries. Every socialist is anti-national; but not every anti-national is a socialist. While the socialist was, and is, presumably subversive, it is clearly possible that there are some persons, presumptively persons of law and order, who were, and are, more subversive than the socialists. They identify themselves with one of the thousand and one categories of the large, too large, Liberal Party. The socialism against which we struggle is driven by a doctrine that has them assuming postures similar to many of those they continue to identify as their enemy.

We have often observed, for example, the socialists, supporters of the Bolshevik regime, the opponents of the family, make common cause with the Popolari, the defenders of private property and the family as an institution. The doctrine that advertised itself the protector of religious interests, and in particular, of national Roman Catholicism, could often ally itself with the pseudo-democracy of the old radicalism, founded on a Masonic base—that is to say, on an abstract rationalism, generically irreligious, and specifically anti-clerical.

These were alliances of equivocal significance and rapid failure, but born of a common principle of evaluation of social and political life and a common doctrine—a doctrine that carried Italian socialist parliamentarianism to the extreme absurdity of fighting to defend parliamentary institutions, the guarantor of a bourgeois liberal society. All of this was the consequence of holding a doctrine that inspired all the gray mediocrity of the fragments of parties to attempt to find whatever way might allow them to form whatever majority, with whatever common denominator, that would permit them to serve as the ruling class. This was the common denominator of democracy.

In our most recent history, who, outside of those in the Camera,[6] could follow all the formations and distinctions and democratic subdistinctions that formed and reformed themselves every day? Every political fragment sought to salvage, with an adjective, who knows what principle—a principle that sometimes seemed resigned to drowning in the vast whirlpool of the substantive: social democracy, liberal democracy, Italian democracy. The first had no reason for not calling itself liberal and Italian, nor the second to refuse the characteristic of being Italian or social, nor the third that of being social and liberal. All of them mixed themselves together under one banner—under which other fractions in the Camera had no reason to enlist, preferring to identify themselves as liberals. All of them were obscurely committed to the proposition that the superior interests of the nation and the State should be subject to those of the various interests, opposed and chaotic—of class, and of categories. In fact, speaking without equivocation, the notion was that the interests of the nation and the State were to be subordinated to the interests of single individuals, who formed themselves, at times, into a majority, and who could therefore exert major pressure on the legislative and governative organs of the State. This is a notion that should have died long since—that should be expunged, whatever the cost, from Italian political life.

This is the individualistic doctrine of the disintegration of the State and of all the moral forces of the nation. Whoever would undertake a careful examination of the most recent history of Italy, would find, among the advocates of that doctrine, some who were more antinational subversives than the socialists. They were among those most responsible for socialist errors—most responsible for the lunatic arrogance that allowed the Socialist Party to prevail against the interests of that very "bourgeois" class the liberals were supposed to represent, particularly during the years that followed the Great War, when every star in the sky of the Fatherland seemed eclipsed....

I have heard it said that Fascism is not a doctrine, that it is innocent of philosophy. It is said that Fascism, opposing itself to the destructive forces of socialist demagoguery with the energy of a moral force that was acknowledged by all, would ultimately return to that traditional liberal doctrine with its healthy conception of the strong State prepared to subordinate to the general interests all the particular interests, and to oppose the arbitrary will of individuals with the inviolable dominance of law. I do not hold to that notion. First of all, let us make a distinction. One should not confound doctrine or philosophy with the systematic expositions that one can put together in well-constructed tracts. I am convinced that true doctrine is that which, rather than found in speeches or in books, is expressed in action, in the personality of human beings, and in the postures that they assume when faced with problems. The very solution of problems is more serious than speculating in the abstract, preaching and theorizing. That is counterfeit theory. Real theory is always practice, a form of life—engaging the human being, certainly not through the blind determinism of instinct, but through knowledgeable convictions and mature purposes enhanced by a secure intuition of the goal sought. This human being is committed to an affirmation or a denial much more meaningful than any clear affirmation or negation of speculative philosophy. What could be a more uncompromising negation of the value of life than suicide? And what would be a more emphatic affirmation of its value than the voluntary sacrifice of the citizen who dies for his Fatherland—for the perpetuation of a concrete ideal of life?

Let us therefore leave books aside and look at the animating ideas—and to the consequent significance of facts that are before us in the great book of history—of far greater grandeur than any elaborate doctrinal exposition....

[If one imagines that Fascism shares some affinity with traditional Italian liberalism that, in its time, appealed to a vigorous, sovereign

State, one must recognize that in our history, there have been a variety of liberalisms.] Of which liberalism does one wish to speak? I distinguish two principal forms of liberalism. For one...liberty is a right; for the other a duty. For one it is gift; for the other a conquest. For one it is [the product of the equality of citizens]; for the other a privilege and a hierarchy of values. One liberalism conceives liberty rooted in the individual, and therefore opposes the individual to the State, a State understood as possessing no intrinsic value—but exclusively serving the well being and the improvement of the individual. The State is seen as a means, not an end. It limits itself to the maintenance of public order, excluding itself from the entirety of spiritual life—which, therefore, remains exclusively a sphere restricted to the individual conscience. That liberalism, historically, is classical liberalism—of English manufacture. It is, we must recognize, a false liberalism, containing only half the truth. It was opposed among us by Mazzini with a criticism, that I maintain, is immortal.

But there is another liberalism, that matured in Italian and German thought, that holds entirely absurd this view of the antagonism between the State and the individual. It was observed that everything of value in the individual has value and pretends to being guaranteed and promoted, by the very fact that it sees the individual as having rights exhibiting universal significance. [If that is the case,] such rights express a will and an interest superior to the will and interest of the individual. It suggests a higher will and a superior personality that is shared and which becomes the ethical substance of the individual.

For such a liberalism, liberty is the supreme end and the norm of every human life—but only insofar as the individual and social education produces it, generating in the individual this common will, that manifests itself as law, and therefore as the State. The State is not a superstructure which imposes itself from without on the activity and initiative of the individual in order to subject him to coercive restriction. The State, in fact, is his very essence, that manifests itself only out of a process of formation and development. As is the case in all instances that form the grandeur and glory of humankind—never a quality that is natural and immediate—this is the result of a constant effort through which the individual, winning against those natural inclinations that invariably drag him down, raises himself to heights of dignity. So understood, the State and the individual are all of a piece. The art of government is to reconcile and identify the two terms, in such a fashion that the maximum of liberty is conciliated with the maximum, not only of exterior public order, but also, and above all, with the sovereignty allowed by law and its necessary agencies. The maximum of liberty always coincides with the maximum force of the State.

What force? The distinctions in this arena are dear to those incapable of being comfortable with this concept of force—which is essential to the State, and therefore to liberty. They proceed to distinguish moral from material force. They distinguish the force of law freely voted upon and accepted, and the force of violence that rigidly opposes itself to the will of the citizen. An ingenuous distinction—even if advanced in good faith! Every force is a moral force—because it always addresses itself to the will. Whatever the argument adopted—from preachments to the truncheon*—its efficacy can be nothing other that to reach within the human being and persuade him to consent.[7] What the nature of this argument should be is not a subject for abstract discussion. Every educator knows that the means of acting on the will must vary according to temperament and circumstances. It is necessary to deal with this issue seri-

---

* This phrase, concerning the truncheon as a "moral force," has engaged the fantasy of many good people, who succeeded in separating it from the context in which it was employed and simply put it in circulation as a motto characteristic of who knows what kind of apology of violence. As a consequence, the phrase has become popular. For many who do not read, or act as though they cannot read, and entertain themselves exclusively with comic newspapers, I have become, for quite some time, the advocate of a "philosophy of the truncheon." It has become a phrase that has generated confusion. I would suppress it if I were not concerned that its suppression would produce equivocations still more annoying. The material force to which I attributed a moral value—the context is clear—is not private force, but the force employed by the State. The State has always been the respository of force that everyone has acknowledged and respected as moral under the concept of the armed force of the State. The State is not armed in order to deliver preachments. The truncheon of Fascist squadrism sought to serve, and served, as the avenging force of the State that had been disrespected and denied by its very constituent central organs. That force was the necessary surrogate of the State in a period of revolution—and according to the logic of all revolutions, the State was in crisis and its force was gradually transferred from its fictive, if legal, organs to its real, if illegal, organs which sought to establish themselves in legality. After the March on Rome, the first problem of Fascism was the suppression of squadrism, which was transformed into the voluntary militia—to become part of the legal armed forces of the State. The truncheon was thus retired to the attic with the hope that it need not ever emerge. It would never emerge if all Italians, Fascist or not, convinced themselves of the necessity and the duty to accord themselves, all together, with the consolidation of the regime that came to fulfill the revolution and thereby to transcend it.

ously. Liberty is not to be found outside the State. The State is not the arbiter of first appeal; it is a living norm, that controls all wills, and realizes in society and in the consciousness of every citizen the irresistible dominance of an iron law...

All of this...is also a doctrine, and arose out of the Great War. We all now possess the sense that Italy has commenced a new phase in its life. Italy has concluded its unification, not just closing an historic period, but rather opening another. We recognize that the Risorgimento was never really effectively concluded. We are now at the real commencement of our national life. We must labor, and arm ourselves, with heart and intellect. We must restore and promote our scientific culture. We must remake our souls. We must acquire a proper consciousness of our mission. It is an imperial mission—not so much in the external world, although the external world requires that Italy, that great mother of peoples, expands in order to live—but more so within Italy itself, to instill in the national consciousness the realization that, as a consequence of our past contribution to civilization and our riches in human potential, we possess not only the right, but the duty to reach out.

Fascism and Culture** (pp. 95-101)

...Sergio Panunzio has affirmed, that we Fascists have need of a defined doctrine. He has insisted that those of us here collected as representatives of Fascist culture must insist that the Fascist Party fully articulate its doctrine.

I would say no, friend Panunzio. The very fact that this reunion, in which many who, with their work and thought, have participated, representing a not insignificant part of the recent history of Italy, has amply demonstrated that the Fascist Party possesses a vast ideal content, without the need to define its doctrine and standardize its delivery. This great reunion, that gives voice to many, expresses a common spirit, a soul that vibrates with a single sentiment, all pursuing a single ideal, the spirit of Fascism.

Great spiritual movements make recourse to precision when their primitive inspirations—what F. T. Marinetti identified this morning as artistic, that is to say, the creative and truly innovative ideas, from which the movement derived its first and most potent impulse—

** A speech delivered at the close of the Congress of Fascist Culture in Bologna, 30 March 1925.

have lost their force. We today find ourselves at the very beginning of a new life and we experience with joy this obscure need that fills our hearts—this need that is our inspiration, the genius that governs us and carries us with it.

Many times the Duce—with profound intuition of Fascist psychology—has affirmed this truth: we all respond to a sort of mystic sentiment. Within that mystic state, clear and distinct ideas hardly formulate themselves. Concepts are not defined; they cannot be expressed in precise propositions nor can the links in the reasoning of a faith be reconstructed....[The] faith that animates us as Fascists—that faith that has given us so much joy and so much satisfaction—which comforted us in our days of pain, when malign efforts were made to weaken our spirit—that faith in which we remained firm—was not an articulated doctrine. It was our very sense, our very being.

I was prepared to speak to the congress of Fascist intellectuals about this trait of Fascism, of which no Fascist more than the intellectual has need to comprehend. In this regard, Professor Piccoli, whom you today have heard speak against intellectualism, has perfect reason. All intellectuals are naturally drawn to that illness of the spirit that is intellectualism. Intellectualism involves that malady as a consequence of which the human being is slowly led to neglect to participate, always and in every fashion, in life, with its joys, its pains, and all its responsibilities. The individual ends with the conviction that he is a simple spectator, located somewhere beyond good and evil. It is an illness to which the human spirit has been exposed in every time and in every nation, but which (and we do well to remember) it has nested for centuries within the spirit of Italians and has corroded and devastated the roots of every generous activity, of every proposal and courageous magnanimity.

....It is necessary to be very clear. Fascism is war against intellectualism. The Fascist spirit is will. It is not intellect. I hope that I will not be misunderstood. Fascist intellectuals should not be *intellectuals*. Fascism combats, and must combat, without respite or pity, not intelligence, but intellectualism—which is, as I have indicated, a sickness of the intellect—which is not the consequence of its abuse, because the intellect cannot be used too much. Rather it derives from the false belief that one can segregate oneself from life, to idle with systems of empty ideas, blind to the tragedy of human beings who work, love, suffer and die. For those who understand, *there* is the place for intelligence—where there is drama, the struggle of man against mystery, the effort to control nature, and intensify life. [One can understand] that intelligence too is will.

Fascism understands that; it disdains culture that is only ornament and adornment. Fascism seeks a culture in which the spirit is armed and reinforced in order to prevail in ever-new battles. That is, and must be, our barbarism—a barbarity of intellectuals. It is a barbarism against science and, above all, against philosophy—but, let it be clearly understood, against the science and philosophy of decadents, of the spineless, of those who forever remain at the window and content themselves with criticism as if [life's struggle] was not their affair!

I would like to assert, parenthetically, one of the major virtues of Fascism is that it obliged, little by little, those who watched from their windows to come down into the street—to identify themselves as Fascists or to oppose it. When all Italians have descended to the street, and think and reflect without any longer retreating to their windows, Italians will once again begin to be the great people they should be.

At this point it is necessary that we do not confuse what should be our culture with the notion of culture as it was understood in the nineteenth century...when the notion of popular instruction first achieved its historic significance. Today, [at this congress] we have perhaps oscillated between these two conceptions—between what I would call the concept of culture without qualifier, equal for all, which is in itself that which it is, something that has in itself an intrinsic value, like golden coin, which can be passed from hand to hand without losing either its proper value or adding to it. It is a kind of material exchange—a transfer from one brain to another, communicable to a few or a great number of those who have need of it. [There is on the other hand, that] which can be said to be Fascist culture—which given its spirit, its fundamental properties, its significance, its values, and because of its potential to serve in a program of life—is different from every other culture....

Yes, there is an objective science, a technical intellectual performance—a unique instrument which one employs to pursue one end, and someone else another. But [those who have normative goals, like] the Roman Catholics appreciate that techniques are not sufficient—they have understood that this "objective" instrument is an abstraction until we know who will employ it—in what program will it be employed? Beyond the objective inanimate instrument there is the living person, with his interests and passions, small and large, particular and universal. For these science serves—because these men think, and are cognitively aware of themselves, of their actions, of goals sought, and of means to be employed....

To those who persist in demanding that science [in order to be objective] must absolutely remove itself from man and his faith, from the profound convictions that sustain his life, and which he cannot, and should not, renounce—tell them that they neither understand what they say, or they are hypocrites. Therefore, in Bologna, a Fascist university arises, with a single faculty of political and social science that is to be the seedbed of a directive leadership of which we have need. It would be the beginning of a new national culture—because every movement of ideas expands by virtue of its own nature, to slowly invest the thought of a nation, to be ultimately reflected throughout the civilized world....

To His Excellency the Honorable Benito Mussolini President of the Council of Ministers (pp. 231-238)

Your Excellency

The Commission nominated by Your Excellency with the Presidential Decree of 31 January 1925, composed of twelve senators, deputies and scholars of political and social issues, in order to study "the problems that today confront the national consciousness and attend the fundamental relationship between the State and all the forces with which it must deal and protect," continues the work begun and already conducted by the Commission of the XV, that in September of last year was charged by the Partito nazionale fascista with the responsibility of studying the problems relative to the State Constitution that arose with the revolution of 28 October 1922. That Commission was, in fact, assembled on the appointed day on which the anniversary of the revoltion was celebrated—and taking its initiative from a communication from His Excellency, Head of the Fascist Party, undertook to formulate the principal themes of the study assigned. Those themes were two: the first dealt with the relationship between the executive and the legislative powers; the other turned on the relations between the State and individual citizens taken both singly and in association (therefore, the State and secret associations, the State and private and public syndicates).

The Commission quickly embarked on an examination of these themes. The Commission decided it would be opportune to select from the second theme the considerations regarding the secret societies—because of the fact that the issue of the secret societies was a matter of not inconsiderable political significance, given the insistence with which the problem engaged the consciousness of the Party out of which the Commission arose. Concerning that argument, it is not necessary for me to recall that as President of the Commission of XV, I had the honor of presenting to Your Excellency the conclusions rapidly concluded in the form of a design of law together with an ample account in which all the historic, juridic and political provisions were clearly provided. That projected law was favorably received by Your Excellency, was presented to Parliament with slight modifications, discussed and approved by the Chamber of Deputies, to be soon a law of the State—that State which Fascism conceives as a regime of superior freedom.

The Work of the Commission of XVIII

The Commission of XVIII, in which almost all the members of the precedent Commission took part, reassembling for the first time on 26 February, approved the problems that were to be studied, and confirmed the appointment of the two subcommissions that had already begun their labors: one presided over by Senator Melodia to consider the first issue [of the relationship between the executive and legislature] and the other presided over by Senator Corradini, who dealt with the second issue above indicated. The number of persons involved grew from fifteen to eighteen in order to incorporate new technical competences. The subcommissions of the Commission of XV were appropriately enlarged.

The two subcommissions and the minor committees formed for specialized work, worked intensively and indefatigably with individual research studies, collegial discussions, with inquiries and interrogatives with experts in order to fulfill their mandate. In the brief life of the Commission, 77 meetings were held in spite of the impediments and difficulties that resulted from the fact that many members were not residents of Rome. Thanks to their alacrity, to their patriotic zeal, and to the absolute selflessness which they applied to their work, and above all to the impressive political experience, knowledge, and skill of all in the materials with which they were required to deal, they could prepare for the plenary Commission, in such a brief period, proposals and illustrations that I am pleased to place before the judgment of Your Excellency. The propositions and relative illustrations of the twenty meetings held by the plenary Commission between 26 February and the 24 of June—after ample and laborious debates, in which every aspect of the single questions were examined with every care and from every point of view—resulted in the schematics of the law and the relations which I now have the honor to present to Your Excellency.

Executive and Legislative Power

The conclusions from the verbal annexes of the meetings have been collected. Here I believe it is only necessary to note that in all the conclusions concerning the relationship between the executive and legislative power, the Commission was in almost unanimous agreement, and that the presentation of the Commission member Barone...expresses that which was the thought of the entire Commission, with the exception of Commission member Gini, whose ideas are to be found in his individual presentation, which is herewith appended. In the conclusions regarding the relationship of the power of the State and the citizens, the Commission divided itself into a majority and a minority. The thought of the majority is contained in the presentation of Commission member Arias, and that of the minority, or at least a part of that minority, is found in the opposed presentation of Commission member Coppola, to which the honorable Mazziotti, Melodia, and Suvich acceded. To that are added the verbal declarations, partially in agreement or analogous, from Commission members Lanzillo and Rossoni, and that contained in the above indicated presentation of Commission member Gini—even though Gini acceded with the majority in terms of the major concepts proposed relative to the second theme—the Corporative Order of the State.

The Corporative Order

It was this issue that divided the Commission—although the Commission was unanimous on another principal point, that of the syndicates. Concerning the syndicates, the Commission was prepared, if asked, that they should be legally recognized, but that the syndicates should not be made obligatory, and that those recognized should be limited to only one for each category.

The issue of the Corporative Order was the most innovative idea considered in the studies and discussions of the Commission. It was therefore to be expected that it would provoke doubts, perplexities, preoccupations, and objections within the Commission. The proponents and adherents of this idea long considered it before taking it up. Some of those who had been most opposed initially were to take it up as advocates. The Commission could hardly hope for an easy and early assent from those who were exposed to these ideas for the first time. One is dealing with a complex idea—and one or another of its elements or aspects might easily be exchanged and confused with other ideas—which the Commission more or less opposed.

Certainly, the Corporative Order is an idea that merits serious and attentive reflection, because in the judgment of the Commission, it is the only one which might indicate how the productive forces of the nation might be effectively dealt with within the ambit of the State's action, rendering the State cognizant of the reality of which it is form, and to which it can neither be indifferent nor separate (as the liberal State tended to be) without losing its material base and with it its organic and organizational potential. Abandoning that idea, there remain only two paths. One might content oneself with the abstract State of individualistic liberalism. But that is not the Fascist State—because Fascism, from its very commencement, has maintained an active political posture, opposing liberal individualism, which it has considered abstract and therefore unreal. Alternatively, one might consider pure Syndicalism. But pure Syndicalism is not the syndicalism of obligatory syndicates—whose very legal recognition implies a principle of obligation to an entity superior to the syndicates, that is to say to a State to which the syndicates would be subordinate. That relationship would contradict the central principle of pure Syndicalism which does not recognize any legitimate power external to the spontaneous and free syndicate. Pure Syndicalism prefers the *de facto* syndicate to the legally recognized syndicate. Pure Syndicalism aspires to absorb the State in itself. In the spontaneous and inevitably fragmentary character and multiplicity of the syndicates, essential unity would be destroyed. Pure Syndicalism is an ideal alternative that is antithetical to the most profound principles and inspirations of the Fascist State.[8]

The Fascist State

The Fascist State is a sovereign State. Sovereign in fact rather than words. A strong State, which allows no equal or limits, other than the limits it, like any other moral force, imposes on itself. The Fascist State does not wish to be a State imposed upon the citizen, rather it wishes to be a State which invests the citizen and informs his conscience. In order to actually shape his consciousness, the State sustains and educates that consciousness; the State recognizes and acknowledges the citizen, to treat him both as what he is, and as that which he should be, historically, economically, morally and politically, with all the fundamental interests that shape him and distinguish him from all others. The Fascist State, in order to penetrate and direct the consciousness of its citizens, wishes to organize them in national unity; a unity possessed of a soul. That unity would manifest itself as a unitary being, possessed of powerful will, and conscious of its own ends.[9] The State has its own ends—that are not those of any particular citizen, nor of any class of citizens, neither in their particularity or in their aggregate, living at any given time within the territory of the juridically defined State. The national unity (which Fascists know and intensely feel) is not something that exists in a determinate time. It has its roots in the past. In the present, it looks toward the future. Today, it lives insofar as it draws vitality from the fruit of centuries, and turns to project itself into an immediate and remote tomorrow. Through its program, it seeks to realize the nation's destiny, the mainspring of its every effort, the very reason for its existence.

The Fascist State is *idea* that vigorously actuates itself. It is an idea and, as such, transcends every present and defined contingent and materialistic form. That is the reason it emphasizes the duties, rather than the rights, of citizens. That is why it solicits them to surpass themselves and anticipate the satisfaction of their own present interests in the future, their own personal advantage in that of the Fatherland, to whom every sacrifice is owed, and from whom every honor is to be awaited.

The Commission, composed of Fascists and classic liberals who view Fascism with sincere sympathy and faith, are inspired with fullness and unanimity of sentiment with respect to that concept, that is the program of the national government and of the Fascist Party.

Toward the Fascist State

None of this is to be understood as an intention, on the part of the Commission, to subvert the Italian State that arose out of the revolution of the Risorgimento. The spirit of Fascism is constructive rather than destructive, and is convinced that the State of the Risorgimento, sustained from the very dawn of revival by the magnanimous faith of the glorious national monarchy, has continued throughout, until the high noon of the victorious and restorative Great War brought the nation to its desired boundaries. That nation, through tradition, is now sacred to every Italian heart, a solid construction to be respected and a solid base upon which the State of the Fascist revolution can be constructed. Thus, in the series of proposals concerning the articulation of the supreme powers of the State, that it is honored to put before the judgment of Your Excellency, the Commission has sought to limit itself to the clearing away all the overgrowth that slowly collected, through parliamentary corruption, around that original and venerated constitutional basis of the Italian State. All that extraneous growth, produced by a corrupt parliamentarianism, gradually overwhelmed that original basis, and made the Constitution serve ends far distant from those of the founders.[10]

It is enough to remember the declaration of the Carl Albert's Minister of Foreign Affairs on the 8 February 1848, when he announced before the representatives of foreign nations, that the new Constitution "was the most monarchial possible"—and then recall the changes in the same Statute that the ministers of His Majesty the King, in that ill-starred year of 1919, considered appropriate—in order to measure the long retrograde distance covered by our institutions from the paths originally intended.

Reform of the Law and Political Practice

The provisions, therefore, suggested by the Commission are limited to particulars, that might appear only accessory to the issue by an inattentive judge. It will certainly not escape Your Excellency that however modest they appear, however cautious in form, inspired by a rigorous realistic criterion of practicability and possibility, these provisions touch very delicate and essential points of constitutional practice on whose restoration may well depend the return of the State to its proper development. That implies as well that the constitution may then serve the ends of the establishment of the anticipated Fascist State.[11] But it is clear to the Commission that all will depend on political custom, that is to say, on the manner in which the constitutional norms are applied. All norms are empty forms that receive significance and concrete value from the spirit with which they are informed. That means that they will receive significance and value only from the force of will with which they are presented, the discipline with which these forms will be observed, and with the faith that animates those who observe them. Given that, Your Excellency—neither the people of Italy nor the Commission of XVIII, can expect true reform except through your efforts, and that of your government. The Commission has only suggested a few instruments that would little serve unless accepted and adopted with committed energy....

Rome 5 July 1925

Notes

1. See Mussolini's comments in "L'Azione e la dottrina fascista dinnanzi alle necessità storiche della nazione," *Opera omnia* (Florence: La fenice, 1971-1974. Hereafter cited as *Oo*), 18, pp. 413-414.
2. The Fascist argument was that the violence of Fascism was the violence of a "virtual" state, a revolutionary state ready to discharge the obligations the established state was incapable of performing. See Mussolini, "Stato, antistato e fascismo," *Oo*, 18, p. 260.
3. See Mussolini's early comments on the "invasion of barbarians," "Avanti sempre o barbari!" *Oo*, 3, pp. 86-87.
4. This was a position assumed by Gentile before there was a Fascism. See Gentile, *Discorsi di religione* (Florence: Sansoni, 1955), p. 26.
5. This is the notion of the "humanism of labor" found explicated in Gentile's last book, *Genesi e strutturà della societa: Saggio di filosofia pratica* (Florence: Sansoni, 1946), pp. 111-112. It is found in the English translation in *Genesis and Structure of Society* (Urbana, Ill.: University of Illinois Press, 1960), pp. 171-172.
6. The lower house of the Italian parliament.
7. It seems clear that Gentile here argues that the violence of Fascism during the period between 1919 and 1922 was the violence of a virtual, revolutionary state. In other places he argues that Fascist violence was simply revolutionary violence. Beyond that, there is the argument that the state, charged with the uplift of its citizens, could not allow error to prevail under any circumstances. This is the central argument that distinguishes liberal democratic and non-democratic political systems. Mussolini acknowledged that distinction by recognizing the affinities

between Marxist-Leninist systems and Fascism. See, for example, Mussolini, "La riforma elettorale" and "Forza e consenso," *Oo*, 19, pp. 195-196, 310. Both Fascism and Marxism-Leninism, as "ideocratic" systems, agreed that it would be immoral to allow "false consciousness" to prevail when it was evident what "true consciousness" was. Extracting consent under such circumstances was a moral responsibility. Gentile provided what is perhaps the best argument for this position in his *Riforma dell'educazione: Discorsi ai maestri di Trieste* (Florence: Sansoni, 1955), the relevant parts of which are translated below.

8. The principle here being examined is that of the "totalitarian" state. The Commission recommended that corporativism be solved within the framework of constitutional law, thereby legitimizing Mussolini's formula of the 28th of October 1925: "Everything within the State, nothing outside the State, nothing against the State."

9. This is political Actualism, articulated before the advent of Fascism; see Gentile, *Discorsi di religione*, pp. 20-23.

10. The original *Statuto* of 1848 did not prescribe any particular form of "responsible government" for the emerging nation. The notion of "responsible government" grew out of parliamentary practice in Italy. Prior to the Fascist revolution, parliamentary government in Italy resembled that of Great Britain and France. In effect, when the Commission of XVIII recommended a return to the *Statuto*, it was recommending that the Italian parliamentary system be neutralized. A return to the *Statuto* restored the right of the monarch to appoint and remove ministers—something that had been made the prerogative of parliament. From the Fascist perspective, a return to the *Statuto* allowed Mussolini (who was appointed directly by the monarch) to rule without parliamentary interference. Ultimately, given the suggested reform, the law gave the Head of the Government the right of veto over all subjects proposed for discussion in either of the two houses of the Italian parliament. Together with that, Mussolini, as Head of the Government, was specifically declared to be "responsible to the King," not parliament, "for the general policy of the government"—a responsibility the King discharged cavalierly until July 1943, when he dismissed Mussolini on monarchial authority.

11. In retrospect, it is clear that the proposed reforms provided the constitutional grounds for the creation of the totalitarian Fascist state. Serving as President of the Commission of XVIII, Gentile was instrumental in the construction of the kind of state he had long since recommended.

Selections from *The Reform of Education* (The Revised 1919 Edition)

Personality and the Problem of Education

Let us attempt to understand clearly what we mean by *concrete personality*—and why the personality which we commonly conceive empirically, the *particular personality*, is an *abstraction*.

Ordinarily, basing ourselves on the obvious testimony of our experience, we believe that the sphere of our moral personality coincides precisely with that of our physical person, measured by the limits of our body. The body constitutes (or at least that is how it is thought) an indivisible unity, in which various parts, through reciprocal correspondence, form a system. The body seems to us to move in space and remains always, as long as it exists, a unity—separated from all other bodies, similar or dissimilar, in a manner in which the one cannot be in the space where there are others and which, in turn, excludes others from occupying its place. One body then, one physical person, one moral personality—that which in each of us is recognized and is affirmed as self-consciousness, as Ego.

I, myself, not only think, but walk. That same being, that Ego that I am when I think, is the same when I walk, resting or moving within space. Just as bodies are impenetrable, so it would seem are personalities, each of which affirms an Ego, the self. That which I am, no one else can be—nor can I confuse myself with another. Those human beings that are most intimately and closely related to me appear completely external to me. Their bodies exist and move outside of mine. My brother, my father, are dead—they have disappeared from this world in which I live and I remain—just as a rock remains if someone removes a rock which rested nearby, or as a mutilated and abandoned pedestal might remain as evidence of a

---

Giovanni Gentile, *La riforma dell'educazione: Discorsi ai maestri di Trieste* (Florence: Sansoni, 1955. First published in 1919.).

statue that has been removed. More than a hundred of us are here collected in this room, but none of us have necessary ties to those around us. Shortly, each of us will go our own way without losing anything of himself, conserving his own proper individuality. Our elders lived on earth before us, and as we arrived, they began to withdraw. Just as they lived before us, we will live and develop our personality without them.

According to these notions, each of us has in himself his own proper being and his own particular destiny. Each makes of himself a center and from that center he constructs, thinking and doing, his own world—a world of ideas, of images, of dreams, of concepts and systems, that are in his brain—a world of values, of desired goods that embellish his life, or evils that he rejects and abhors, all of which have their origins in his will, in his character, in his manner of conceiving and coloring the world.

What does the pain or pleasure of others mean to me? And what does the thought of Aristotle and Galileo mean to me if I do not know them, if I do not read their books, and remain unfamiliar with their science? And of what importance are our most exalted thoughts, and the songs that arise from the depths of our soul, to the stranger that we encounter on the street—who does not even spare us a glance? Another's heroism brings us no glory, nor does the heinous deed of the most violent criminal—while it may horrify us—disturb our conscience. Each of us has his own body and his own soul. Each of us, in effect, remains himself whatever others may be.

This concept that we customarily apply when speaking of our personality—and which forms the basis of every thought about our practical, interpersonal, life—is a conceptual abstraction. In fact, conceiving our being in that manner, we see only one side, allowing the other to escape. We allow to escape that which is spiritual, human, that is to say all that which is really and peculiarly ours. I shall not here investigate how the human personality might have two such diverse aspects, or from which profound source these two manifestations so opposed might spring—so different that the one appears to be the negation of the other. For our present purposes, it is enough to now reflect, and firmly persuade ourselves that, together with particularity, there is another element of our person—an element that is opposed to every particularity, in which we find our most profound nature, wherein we cease to find ourselves in stark opposition to everyone else, and in which we discover ourselves in all others as they are or as we wish them to be.

In order to fix your attention on this more profound aspect of your interior life, I wish to employ an illustrative example—an example that can be understood as a component of the concept of nationality: *language*. Language, I must remind you, does not belong, *per se*, to nationality; it has a universal character that becomes national when a particular personality, by acting, employs it for determinate purposes. One must understand that to see language only as a constituent element of our particular personality is to deal with abstractions.

That our personality contains, among its constituent elements, language, is obvious. We employ language not only to speak to others but to ourselves as well. And to speak to oneself means to deal with one's own ideas, one's own soul and, in sum, with oneself—to have consciousness of oneself as philosophers are wont to say, and therefore to possess self-control, a clear comprehension of our acts, and of all that which stirs within us. It means living not after the manner of a dumb beast, moved by sense and instinct, but as a human being, a rational animal. No one can imagine that a human being can think, have consciousness of self and reason, without expressing himself, and express himself, before all else, to himself. Man has been defined as a reasoning animal. One might also define him as an animal that speaks. That is a truth known already to Aristotle.

Man, understood as an animal that speaks, is not man in general—something that never was—but real man, that man who is each one of us: the historic, existing, and actual human being. He would be a man who does not speak a generic language, but a specific language. That is how I speak, and I cannot but speak a given language, the Italian language. And I exist, that is, I affirm myself, I realize myself, thinking as this personality which I am, in so far as I speak, in my own language. *My* language, as I said, the *Italian* language. Herein lies the problem.

If I were not to speak, or were I to speak otherwise than I do, I would not be me. This manner of expressing myself is therefore an intrinsic characteristic of my personality. All of you, everyone, could say as much. But this language which makes me what I am, and which belongs and is intrinsic to me, could it serve me, could I make it flesh of my flesh, if it, mine as it is, was closed within me as the fibers of my being are closed within my body without having anything in common with any other part of the matter with which I coexist in space? My language, in short, could it really be my language if it was exclusively mine, belonging to what we have identified as my particular and empirical personality?

A simple reflection is all that is necessary to demonstrate that my language, which serves as a light that illuminates every angle and renders visible every movement and every sense of my thought, can only so serve because that language is not exclusively my own. It is the same language that allows me to read and understand the authors of our antiquity who, like me, are "Italians." I read about Francesca da Rimini and Count Ugolino, and they are there in my own spiritual emotions. I read of golden-haired Laura and of the beautiful Angelica—the desire of gentlemen and the unhappy lover of the youthful Medoro. I read of the manner with which the Florentine secretary, Machiavelli, with his acute speculations, sought to establish the principalities and the State of Italy. I read of the many loves, pains, discoveries, and sublime concepts that did not have their origins in me but among those great masters. Once having been given expression by those masters, the loves, sorrows, discoveries, and sublimities acquired a place in the imagination, the intellect, and in the hearts of Italians and have thereby become the treasures of our literature, bringing light to the life of language, varied and restless, but forever the same. It is a language that I learned as an infant from the sainted lips of my mother, and which I continued to appropriate, studying and reflecting over books and through conversations, exchanging ideas and sentiments daily, over the years, with those of my community. My language is the language of all those, living or dead, that forever unites us, you with me, with our own people.

Should I wish to separate myself, with this language, from this glorious community—should I desire to demonstrate that this language is uniquely mine—I would have produced the exception that proves the rule. For surely a person may devise a cryptic language, a jargon, a cipher. Jargon and ciphers, in fact, are adopted, in order to communicate secrets among a selected number of persons. The groups they form are artificial. The "language" employed, nonetheless, is intrinsically a language in that it imitates nature—it reflects the immanent law of language, which is that language can be anything but secret. Rather, like all the products of the spirit, language intrinsically involves a community, and aspires toward the universal. A cryptic language is possible only because it can be translated into the common language. If one were to give the cipher to the cryptographer—by virtue of the same ingenuity that allowed the cipher to be created—a translation would be forthcoming. He breaks the artificial form and allows the encrypted language to flow back into a language that is intelligible to all who speak the same national tongue.

Moreover, every word, in its original novelty, when it emerges from the inspired breast of the poet who creates it, is something like jargon—it belongs, in a real sense, to the poet who fashioned it. Until the meaning of the word is revealed—the word could be considered part of a private language. And yet, if one looks more deeply, one uncovers its roots in the common language. One may speak to oneself, but with the anticipation of an audience. One speaks a word that must eventually be intelligible to others if it is to serve any purpose. In the circumstances in which he finds himself, one might use a word because it is appropriate—with the anticipation that anyone similarly circumstanced would use that word and no other. His word is the word appropriate to the circumstance. Should the person be a poet, a serious person, who expressed a term particularly apt, a word that is not jargon, he first speaks the language of his people—and then of humanity at large—because what he has to say engages those of many nations, having many languages, including that of the poet.

Language, in sum, is a *universal* activity, that unites human beings rather than dividing them. It achieves that universality through the agency of the family community, the city, the region and that of the nation—together with many other forms of intimate aggregation and fusion that we find in history.

A person's nationality may or may not be a function of his language. That can only be the product of his *will* through which he makes and remakes himself every moment of his life. But can that will, that makes of each of us what he is, be his own will—exclusively his own? Or is the will itself, like one's national language—while not a common legacy—an activity shared in common in so far as one cannot live one's life except by living the common life of the nation?

Abstractly speaking, we always find ourselves affirming that mine is a particular will. But insofar as each of us is capable of distinguishing between empty words and will, we recognize the difference between the will that would be will and is not, a velleity—and a genuine, effective will that does not content itself with expressions of intentions, plans, and sterile desires—but acts, and by its action, renders itself valuable, giving evidence of its reality. We are each responsible for what we are—not because of that which we wish to be, but for that which, in fact, we actually want to be. Velleity is the expression of a will directed toward a goal that is absolutely or relatively impossible to achieve. Real will finds expression in that which can be accomplished.

When is it the case that my will is effective and really wills? I am a citizen of my *State*, that has a power, a will that manifests itself as *law*—law that it is necessary to obey. Transgression of the law, in a State truly possessed of power and will, will inevitably result in the punishment of the transgressor—the application of that very law that the transgressor has refused to recognize. The State is sustained by the inviolability of its laws—those blessed laws of the Fatherland that Socrates, as Plato tells us, taught us to venerate. I, as a citizen of my State, am bound by its laws insofar as I should choose to transgress them I would be choosing the impossible—like attempting to speak a private language. Should I choose the impossible, I would be indulging in vain velleities, in which my personality, far from realizing itself, would be impaired and dispersed. Conforming my will to the law recommends itself; I will what the law wishes.

It is not important if, materially or explicitly, positive law does not occupy the entire sphere of my activity and leaves to the internal dictates of my particular conscience the determination of the major part of my conduct. This same delimitation between the juridical and the moral, between that which depends on the law of the State and that which turns on the ethical conscience of the individual, is a distinction that results from the will of the State—there is no preexisting limit to which the constitutive and legislative power of the State must limit itself. Positively or negatively, through command or compliance, all of our conduct is subject to the will by which the State establishes its concrete reality.

There is more. The will of the State reveals itself not only in law (as positive law). The State leaves to private initiative every form of undertaking for which that initiative is appropriate and sufficient without the intervention of sovereign and directive power. It leaves to private management its freedom until such time as private man-

Selections from *The Reform of Education* (The Revised 1919 Edition) 83

agement ceases to be effective. Even when the will seems to be self-motivated, free of every explicit constraint of common law, in fact, that will wishes only that which the sovereign State wishes that it wills. The reality is that a seemingly autonomous will is actually the will of the State not expressed in terms of positive legislation—there being no need of such expression where compliance is automatic. The essence of the law is not in its expression, but in the will that is its source, observes it, and assures conformity to it. The essence of the law is in the will that wishes it. It follows that the law is thus not absent even when it does not take the form of positive law.

In conclusion, I, as the citizen I am, want that which I want; but when one inspects what I want, that which I want coincides precisely with that which the State wants—my will is the will of the State.

And if that were not the case? If I were to accept such an hypothesis, the very soil beneath my feet would give way. For it would mean that I exist, but the State does not. It would be to insist that the State does not exist in which I was born and which protected me even before my birth, which sustained me and fostered this communal life in which I have always lived, which constitutes my spiritual substance, the world upon which I depend with the faith that, while constantly changing, will never fail. I could—it is true—refuse to acknowledge this intimacy by which I am joined and fused with this majestic will that is the will of Italy. I could balk and rebel against its laws. In doing so, as I have indicated, I would be indulging in a velleity. My personality, my very being, incapable of transforming the will of the State, would be overcome and suppressed.

[That some would choose to violate positive law and common practice is probably a consequence of the fact that some] imagine that they could separate themselves from all else, rejecting that common will and every law—and within the vast expanse of their thought, at the height of an inaccessible summit, proudly proclaim the uniqueness of their Ego—and its will. In a certain sense, this notion appears confirmed by the fact that my personality, like the personality of everyone else, seems capable of conceiving itself in just such fashion. The evidence is deceptive. Is it the case that I can act as a unique being [with a unique will]? Or is it rather that a universal power acts through me as my personal will [and my egoism deceives me]?

Let us reflect. When we morally obey the law, sincerely and effectively, we make the law our own, and our behavior is the direct result of our convictions—our convictions guide our conduct. Every time we act, the condition is that we look within—to determine if our act is an act which should be done. The saint that makes God's will his own, recognizes in his norms a necessity equal to that seeming necessity felt by the sinner. The sinner's sense of moral necessity is mistaken and destined to end in failure. Every delinquent violates the law because he has fashioned a law unto himself in contrast to the laws of the State. He thus proposes his own State—different from that which historically exists. (The existing State exists for good reason. The delinquent will subsequently learn to acknowledge those reasons.) From the point of view the delinquent chooses, his act is reasonable. The transgressor imagines that his reasoning has a universality that would make his act reasonable to anyone similarly circumstanced. The transgressor imagines that his will is not particular, but universal. Giving expression to that will, he would establish new laws in place of the old. He would construct a new State on the ruins of the old. Thus does a tyrant destroy the liberty of the Fatherland, substituting one State for the other—thus does a rebel—assassinating the tyrant and successful in his undertaking—restore liberty. If the rebel is unsuccessful, he is vanquished and his will returns to conform itself to that of the State he failed to overthrow.

That is the way it is. My true volition is the will of the State acting as a particular will—in fact, my true volition is the will of the world of nations in which my own State coexists with the others, upon which it acts, and which act upon it. My true volition is that of the world. My will is not only my own; it is a universal will. It is a form of universality embodied in a political community in which single individuals associate and unite themselves in a higher individuality historically distinct from other political entities that are similar.

Thus we can say that we are prepared to recognize that our personality, in abstraction, is particular; but it realizes itself *concretely* in the form of a universality, which at one stage is national. This concept of a concrete, because universal, personality is of primary importance for those of us who live in the schools and who have made the education of humanity our life's purpose and mission.

Around the concept of personality, one of the major problems of education turns. It is the problem that has forever been a preoccupation from the time when reflection on education began. Since one can say that from the time there have been human beings, there has been education, so can one say that there has always been this con-

Selections from *The Reform of Education* (The Revised 1919 Edition)   85

cern. Education, we must remember, is not a fact, if by fact we mean, as we should, something that has happened, or will probably happen, or must predictably happen by virtue of the regularity of the law which governs it. No, all of you, in your consciousness as educators, feel it: the education of which we speak, which interests us, for which we work, and which we seek to improve, is not something fixed and finished—not something that takes place in accordance with the laws of nature. Education involves free action, the vocation of our souls, the duty of humankind, an act which, more nobly than any other, allows the human being to actualize his superior nature. Animals do not educate themselves even when they raise their young. They do not form families, ethical organisms in which differentiated members [consciously] organize themselves into systems. Human beings, on the other hand, freely and consciously, acknowledge our children as we do our parents and brothers as extensions of ourselves. In such circumstances we consciously develop our respective personalities and seek to assist in the development of the personality of others. In the human family, in society, in the city, in any community, we constitute but one collective spirit, with common needs that are satisfied through individual activity within a social matrix.

If human beings are said to be political or social animals, one can also say that they are animals that educate. We do not only educate the young, our own young, but if education is spiritual action upon the spirit, we educate whenever and wherever we interact, in our families and outside our families, within and outside the school, to the extent that with us they form a society—not only minors who are under tutelage attending school or the workplace where their abilities, their character and their culture is increased and improved—but adults as well, mature and even elderly adults, because there is no living person that does not learn something every day, and does not benefit from human contact. Human education never ceases.

Like every form of his activity, the human being does not educate by instinct or by abandoning himself to natural impulse. He is conscious of what he does—and is aware of what he does in terms of education, to direct it more efficiently toward his goal, without a waste of energy and to attain the best results possible. Human beings reflect.

You recognize that pedagogy is not an invention of pedagogues and pedants who intervene with their theories and elucidations in this blessed work of love that has parents united with children, the masters with the unlettered, and human beings with each other, in order to extend a hand to help, so that all may rise together from one height, to another still higher, more elevated. Before the word "pedagogy" was coined, as is often the case, the term had a referent. Before there was the term "science" with its title and its university chair, there was that which is the life of science and therefore the rationale for the chair. There was the intense reflection of humankind, which in accordance with the divine injunction "know thyself," became conscious of his own labor, never to allow himself to be simply the object of events, but to consider everything a problem requiring conscious solution. What the animal does unerringly through infallible instinct, human beings undertake to consider everything with conscious intelligence, and seek and explore, through a fallible process, to achieve the good—not infrequently failing but always picking oneself up to achieve a higher grade of cognition and of art. Human education is human, therefore, not a fact, prefabricated and finished, but action. Action always remains a problem for us—that we proceed to solve and which we must keep solving forever.

This is an intuitive truth confirmed by experience, at least as long as we retain that primitive freshness as educators, not to succumb to routine and simple habit—as long as we remain capable of seeing in the face of every new student a unique soul, different from all the others with whom we have dealt, and different from himself with each passing day. This will be true as long as we are capable of assuming our tasks thrilled with anticipation, ready for revelations that are new, ready for new experiments, for new difficulties, feeling the movement and the rush of life which renews itself in us and around us with each new generation we encounter and which must ultimately leave us—to go out and face life and death. We teachers must forever make recourse to that which is beyond and above us so that we never succumb to that sense of routine which would have us always repeat the same story, within the same walls, all with the same corpulence, those same tired and distracted faces—all indistinguishable one from the other! We must remember that we are educators as long as we recognize every instance of our work as new—and education as always a problem that demands ever new solutions.

Finally, the problem of problems in the field of education, both in antiquity and at the present, is this: the educator represents to his students the universal in the form of historically determined scientific thought, customs, law, art, religious creeds, not in so far as they are the thought, the customs, the law, the art and the creed of the teacher, but in so far as they are those of humanity, in his country and in his epoch. And the student is that particular individual who, having entered into the educative process, becomes subject to the constraints of school, and thereby ceases to enjoy the liberty of his own research and formulation of his own patrimony or spiritual character. The student bends beneath the influence of education in general and thereby to common law. That is the source of the old repugnance to the constraints of education, and the rebellion which time and time again rises against the presumed right of the educator to intervene in the spontaneous development of a personality in search of its own path. The intervention is made on the pretext that the educator is possessed of superior value by virtue of his beliefs, his doctrine, his tastes, and his moral conscience.

It is clear that, on the one hand, education is occupied with the development of liberty for humankind. To educate is to produce human beings—and a human being is worthy of the name when he is master of himself, with the initiative and the responsibility for his own acts, with conscience and discernment with respect to those ideas he takes up, professes, affirms, propagates—that is to say all that he does, says and thinks. We believe that we have educated our children when they are grown and provide evidence that they no longer have need of our guidance and counsel. Our work as teachers is considered to be at an end when our students speak our language, and they are capable of speaking both appropriately and creatively. The goal of education is to produce [the conditions conducive to the exercise of true] liberty.

On the other hand, to educate signifies to act on the spirit of others, and not abandon them to themselves. The educator must awaken an interest in the student that he might have never sensed—turn him to a goal the value of which he might not have otherwise recognized—guide him along a path that he might not have ever trod—thereby giving him something of ourselves, to fashion a character, a mind, a will, that is something of our own spiritual substance. In such fashion, whatever the student does as a consequence of our education, would be, in some sense, our own doing. In such fashion education does not result in making the human being free, in fact it destroys in the student that liberty with which he entered the world. How often do we ascribe to the family and the environment in which the human being is raised, the responsibility or the merit for the actions of an adult?

This is the form in which the problem characteristically presents itself. The spirit of the educator vacillates between the desire and the zeal to care and guide the development of the student directly and rapidly—and the fear of suffocating creativity, to constrain with his presumptuous labor the spontaneous and personal direction of the spirit, to impose on the individual a garb that is not his own—to crush him under the weight of a leaden cape.

The solution to this problem is to be found in the *concrete* concept of the individual personality—and we will seek it again in what follows. We remind the reader that our solution cannot be expected to eliminate every difficulty—like a key that opens all doors.

I have already argued that education is always problematic, and we can never claim to have the solution to all its problems—liberating ourselves from thought. Our solution is only one way, along which every person of judgment and good will might time and again solve his own problem. The problem of education will always reappear in new forms, and requires a continuous development to be found in the progressive interpretation of the concept in which we maintain that one can find his solution. We all recognize that no power of thought, at any given time, frees us from thinking, thinking always, thinking ever more intensively.

The Fundamental Antinomy of Education

Please follow me in a more precise, more formal determination of that which I have referred to as the old and always new problem of education. That problem is identified as an "antinomy"—a conflict of two contradictory affirmations each of which appears both true and irrefutable. The two affirmations are the following: (1) the human being that is the object of education is, and should be, free; (2) education violates the liberty of human beings. One might also say: (1) education presupposes the liberty of the human being; (2) education prescinds from the liberty of human beings and works in a fashion that would divest him of his entire liberty.

All the propositions are not to be considered approximate but the exact expression of an irrefutable truth. When the talk is of liberty one should understand liberty full and absolute. When it is said that there is a negation of liberty we mean that education as such, and as much and as far as it educates, annihilates the liberty of the student.

First of all, what is this liberty that is attributed to human beings? Each of us possesses some obscure, if insistent, conception of it. Each of us, even if unfamiliar with the discussions that have attended philosophers' treatment of free will over the centuries, still have had some experience with the difficulties that surround the use of the claim that human beings enjoy free will and are really free. On the other hand, each of us has had the direct experience in life that convinces us, with a faith that is instinctive and irrepressible, that liberty survives all the doubts and negations.

By liberty we mean the peculiar power of human beings to make of themselves what they would be, and therefore to initiate a series of events in which, and through which, they act. Within nature we conceive of all the facts in such a manner that phenomena are colligated among themselves in a universal, complex system in which no single fact constitutes the first cause because each fact is seen as having an antecedent cause or constitutes, in any event, the necessary condition of its intelligibility. The condensation of aqueous vapor in the clouds leads to rain, but vapor would not condense were it not for changes in temperature—and that would not happen had it not been for antecedent meteoric circumstances.

We believe, on the other hand, that the actions of an individual find their source in the individual himself. If we observe that the action of the individual does not have its origin in himself, but is the result of some extraneous cause affecting his character or, momentarily, his will—the action could not possess the moral value that makes it properly human, to be distinguished from the instinctive activity of the beast, or the effects of the brute power of inanimate nature.

On occasion we deny humanity to an individual, and we observe in his conduct an explosion of brutal impulse, ferocious cruelty and irrationality—moments when terms of approbation or condemnation are entirely inappropriate. On those occasions we do not even appeal to reason in dealing with such a person. To defend ourselves against his violence, nothing remains to us but violence—the same weapon that we employ against the most savage animals and the blind forces of nature. At such a point, the human being in us refuses to recognize the human being in the offending individual. A human being is considered such when we believe that he can be influenced through arguments that appeal to reason and sentiment, properties peculiar to, and the prerogatives of human beings. The reason and sentiment to which we appeal constitute the particular essence of the human personality. They cannot be imparted from without, but belong to the individual—at least in germ—at his very birth, and must subsequently be cultivated by himself. They are something that render a human being capable of consciously controlling his actions. The individual must understand his own actions in two senses—to know what it is that he does, and appreciate how his actions will be judged. In such a fashion, all the material causes which influence him have nothing to do with his behavior, which he must consider, as a human being, only in terms of his own reasoned judgments. Is there anything more natural than to react with vengeance to an affront and to arm oneself with hatred for one's enemy? Nonetheless, from the standpoint of morals, a human being is a human being in so far as he is capable of resisting the powerful passions that drive him to meet evil with evil and hatred with hatred. The human being *should* pardon, *should* love the enemy that has done him injury. Only when he is capable of appreciating the beauty of pardon and love, will he no longer do that which is *naturally* expected of him—he ceases to be a *natural* thing and lifts himself to that superior realm, that is the domain of morality, wherein the human being must progressively exhibit his humanity. Whether or not human beings are capable of so much, we admit every human being into the society of humans with the presupposition that they are capable of so conducting themselves. We expect the human being to be [capable of freedom of choice and] not the plaything of causes external to his will and personality—that interior core from which his personality reaches out to us to affirm itself. We make these demands on him, commending him when he displays the capacity to resist those external forces which would shape his behaviors, and we condemn him when he fails. We blame him only because we are convinced that he should have had the strength to resist those extraneous material forces—and that he lacked the power to resist.

It is of no significance that we sometimes reduce the measure of blame as a consequence of compassion, or out of the humble recognition that human beings are weak. There forever remains within us the reprove, even if unspoken, of his weakness, with the conviction that he might have done more, much more, and that he should do everything possible in the future, with our help, to victoriously oppose himself to evil—and to do his duty. We cannot abandon the unhappy person, who because of his weakness—his craven cowardice or the unthinking violence of the brute—does evil. Our obligation is to care for him and help him in the belief that he can be redeemed—that he is, basically, a human being like us who has within himself the potential for a life superior to that in which he languishes.

There is a pseudo-science that, on the basis of a superficial and nonrepresentative observation, maintains that certain forms of delinquency are the consequence of determinants over which men have no control. They are fatally condemned to remain deaf to that voice of duty that rises up irresistibly, with the least appeal from other humans, from the very profundity of their being. These are the theses of the recent school of criminal anthropology that has provided international fame to some Italian authors. Much of their luster has now faded, since practically speaking, their observations concerning the pathological quality of delinquency have not helped in the treatment of delinquency, which responds more effectively to therapies that are more rational.

Their doctrine corresponds to those systems which, at all times are driven by materialistic motives (which may at times assume religious or teleological garb), that deny human beings that power, which is identified as liberty, and condemn them to behave as small particles in the immense sea of universal determinism, perpetually moved and agitated together with an impersonal mass of water. What power could each particle have to resist the force of the wave that carried it forward? Thus human beings, every human being, from the time of his birth and his death, confined in the midst of all the being of nature, feeling the effects of all these concurrent factors, would be driven and tossed from moment to moment by the powerful currents immanent in the universe. At times, the individual may imagine that his consciousness might lift itself above those forces, to resist them, to arrest them and dominate them, to employ them in the service of his own destiny. But his belief is a delusion, itself the fatal effect of the unconscious play of those representations that are themselves the effects of external forces.

It is not our purpose here to criticize those arguments with which, in the systems to which we have referred, it is held that one can imagine human beings without liberty. For our present purposes, one observation is enough to truncate the entire discussion. A great

German philosopher (Immanuel Kant), who conceived a notion of science and reality which treated science as object, to the exclusion of a way to treat reality as a place in which human beings could have liberty, made a place for liberty—irrespective of all the difficulties that science encounters in the effort to make a place for it—because finding such a place is a *postulate* of our moral conscience. What that signifies is that whatever our ideas and whatever the theories of science, we have also a conscience, which imposes on us a law—a law which, without having been promulgated and established by an exterior force, is for us absolute—a moral law. It is a law that does not require a speculative rationale. In fact, the arguments of philosophers are only of relative service in its support—since the moral law arises spontaneously from the very depths of our spirit, and demands from our will, even from the most uncultivated among us, unconditional respect. The fact of the matter is, what could the significance of the word *duty* be, if the human being could only do that which his nature, or worst still, what external nature, compels him to do? When it is said that someone *must*, that implies that he *can*. The indefensible conviction we have that we can properly be expected to perform our duty, implies with equal certainty that we can perform that duty: that is to say, it implies we are free to do, or not do, our duty.

However important, such a reflection is not sufficient to solve our problem. One might argue that this certitude we have of a moral consciousness, and the notion that we are charged with a duty from which we cannot escape—could that not be an illusion? Nothing makes such a thought self-contradictory. Skeptics and naturalistic philosophers accept just such notions.

Liberty is not only necessary to sustain our conception of moral obligation—liberty is not only the condition (*ratio essendi*) of moral law, as imagined by Kant. Liberty is the necessary condition for the life of the spirit. The materialist who would believe that he might reject freedom as the condition of morality—imagining it possible to continue to think, renouncing any thought of objective value, or in the reality of a moral law—deludes himself. Without liberty human beings could no longer speak of duty—in fact, they could no longer speak—much less articulate their materialistic views. The denial of liberty is literally unthinkable.

Some brief reflections will make this evident. We speak to others or to ourselves, in so far as we think, saying something and formulating propositions. Let us suppose that the ideas we have in mind (as it is sometimes alleged) are unobserved. Such ideas would not have presented themselves to consciousness, just as objects toward which we do not turn our gaze, would remain unknown to us. Every object, that is to say, every thought we have in mind, is not thought unless it is in mind. We must be there, in the form of mental activity. Each of us must be there as a thinking human being, the subject who is prepared to affirm the object. Thought consists precisely in the affirmation of the object by the subject. It must be noted that the subject, that is to say the human being, must be free in making such affirmation in thought, just as he must be free in any action which is truly his and thereby truly human. We expect of a human being that he be responsible for his thought—just as he is responsible for his actions. We often make persons responsible for their thoughts when we judge that they ought not think such thoughts. We thereby demonstrate that we are convinced that the thought of each of us is not only the logical consequence of certain premises, or an effect of a psychic mechanism put in motion by the universal mechanisms of which the individual psyche finds itself a part. The thought of the individual is not subject to premises he cannot modify once they are accepted. We are masters of our thoughts—illustrated not only by the vigor with which the human personality pursues the demands of a difficult and arduous practical life, but also the agility, readiness, assiduity, and dispassionate love of truth, with which we prosecute our research for the truth.

It has been said that human cognition has its own moral value, and that the will intervenes in the work of the intellect. Such a distinction is perilous. Whether we call it will or intellect, the activity which makes us what we are, by which we actualize our personality—it is certain that it is conscious and discriminating activity, not like a weight falling on an object. Our conscious activity involves conscious freedom. Just as every action turns to the good because something appears good as opposed to evil, thus every cognition is an affirmation of a truth, that is or seems to be such, in opposition to error and falsehood. Without the antithesis of good to evil, there would be no moral action. Similarly without the antithesis of truth to falsity there would be no knowing. The antitheses [between good and evil and truth and falsehood] imply choice and thereby a freedom to choose.

Should we deny the freedom to choose, abandoning the human being to the causes which act on him, the consequence would be that no distinction could be made between good and evil or between that which is true and that which is false. Thus, the materialist, who would deny freedom to the human being would not only find himself without a basis for attributing value that the moral conscience assigns to the good—but equally without the grounds for attributing value to truth. He must convince himself that he has no reason for thinking what he does—rendering the entire process impossible.

The negation of freedom leads to just such absurdity—to the impossible notion that this impossible thought, which is being thought—is a thought which cannot admit of being thought. The human being in so far as he thinks affirms his faith in liberty—and every effort he makes to extirpate such a faith from his soul, is its most flagrant confirmation. Properly understood, this observation is sufficient to secure the irreducible foundation on which human liberty rests.

Nor is it the case that the liberty necessary for human beings to be human, is or can be, as some have thought, a relative liberty, governed by certain conditions. A conditional liberty is [tantamount to] slavery. That is the central issue. To admit a relative liberty is to open the issue to questions of how much or how little liberty there might be. But freedom is either absolute or it is nothing. Matter is not free—every material thing is not free, precisely because it is limited. The spirit—in every one of its acts—is free because it is infinite, not relative to any thing because it is absolute.

Once the spirit is limited, liberty is annihilated. The slave is not free is so far as his will is circumscribed by limits imposed upon it by his master. The human spirit is not free in the face of nature, because nature confines it to narrow limits, within which only that development is permitted that nature itself allows. It is rather a development to which nature condemns the spirit, because the spirit is thus confined to a circumscribed range of activity. The lower animal is not free because even if its behavior appears to share rationality with human beings—it follows a rectilinearity and a pre-established line of instinctual conduct that does not permit any individual originality or creativity. Whoever speaks of limit, alludes to that which limits and that which is limited—a necessary relationship the one with the other. It is impossible for the limited to escape the consequences of that relationship—which means, in sum, that it is impossible for the limited to be everything—that it must remain within its limits, observing the inviolable laws of its nature. The necessity that ties every natural being to the laws of its own nature is that which renders each that which it is—a wolf is born a wolf, a lamb a lamb—that is the hard determinism of natural beings. That is the determinism from which man is ransomed by the powerful force of his liberty.

Thus the sculptor, in the fervor of divine inspiration, seeks marble, out of which his chisel might form, in the very bosom of nature, the idol of his dream. He searches and fails to find that which he seeks—and his chisel can only remain idle. The artist is frustrated in his effort by an extrinsic natural impediment—which seems to limit his creative power. When we consider what the artist creates in the statue, the living image he has imposed on the white marble, we recognize in it nothing material, only the idea, the sentiment, the soul of the artist—the apparent limits to the creative power of the artist disappear. There is no longer the fantasy of the artist, and then his arm, his hand, and his chisel, and the block of stone on which he labors—we perceive only the creative fantasy, taking wing in that infinite world of the artist, with his arm, hand and marble and his universe entirely different from the universe in which men live who quarry marble in the hills, transport and sell it.

There is a point of view from which the spirit appears limited, and therefore servant of the conditions in which its life is spent. There is also a higher point of view to which we must accede if we would discover our liberty. Should we distinguish—as is common in psychology—between the soul, body, sensation, movement, thought and the external world, we really would have no way of conceiving the spirit as anything other than as something conditioned by the physical externalities to which its internal determinations must somehow correspond. It is impossible to see without eyes and without light. It is equally impossible not to see when one has eyes and objects are illumined—and given the wave frequencies, it is impossible not to see one or another color. The objects seen will determine our thoughts, and according to that which is thought, our volition will be shaped, to forge in us this or that character. We shall be this or that human being in conformity with prevailing circumstances. In such a conception, a human being is made up of contingencies, a child of his place and time, of the society around him. He cannot be the product of his own making—but of everything else—his time, his place, his environment.

But there is that superior point of view, to which I have already alluded, that one must attain if one would really understand this stupendous human nature that was revealed to our consciousness by Christianity, and which has increasingly manifested itself in the course of the modern era, making the human being aware of his own dignity, superior to that of nature which he increasingly subjects to his will the more he achieves understanding. Nature is bent to his will and employed to achieve goals which he chooses. Human beings do not cease their efforts irrespective of the obstacles nature places in their path.

Whoever says that there are two things—the soul and the body, two things, one outside the other—does not consider that these two things are distinguished in thought by thought itself, that is to say the distinction is made in the soul itself. The soul is more true than the body because the soul thinks, and therefore the soul thinks and reveals its nature by its intrinsic acts. Things reveal themselves only as the objects of thought, as a thing thought, and as things thought may be delusions, figments of imagination (*ens rationis*). Many things thought have shown themselves to be inconsistent, without substance—fictions. Whoever speaks of sensation and movement which generates or conditions, in whatever manner, sensation, forgets that sensation itself is a determination of consciousness, just as movement, which is something one may also encounter in consciousness—[the difference being that one thinks of movement] when one thinks of the displacement of things in space.

Everything must remain within [the circumference of] consciousness. There is no way to escape that reality—because if we would choose to say that outside or around consciousness there is the brain, which is enclosed in the cranium, which in turn is enveloped by a space filled with luminous air and populated by a congress of flora and fauna—we would have to concede that all of that is conceived in thought, within consciousness, to which it remains external and dependent. Think—keep in mind the indestructible substance of your thought—and from the center of that thought, of which we are the subject, advance, proceed forward, always advancing toward an ever receding horizon. Is there any point at which one would be prepared to say, "Here my thought ends and here begins something else?" Thought cannot stop other than before a mystery. But having thought of that mystery, thought transforms it in the thinking, and proceeds, after a pause, without ever really stopping.

That is the life of the spirit. It is for that reason we have spoken of the spirit as universal. In its travels through the infinite, it finds nothing other than that which it fashions spiritually. In this life, when viewed from within, and not abstracted, conceived with a materialistic imagination, the spirit, we reiterate, is free because infinite.

Does education presuppose this kind of liberty on the part of the student? Certainly, because the student is conceived of as educable—and the student would not be educable if incapable of thinking (and understanding that which he is told). And to think, we have argued, is what freedom means.

Not only is freedom presupposed by the educator, but it is the very thing he seeks to develop in trying to enhance the capacity to think and every other manner of spiritual undertaking. The development of thought is the development of reflection, of man's control over his ideas, over the content of his own consciousness, over his own proper being in relationship to every other being. The educator's work, in effect, is the development of liberty. Someone has said that education, in point of fact, consists in the liberation of the individual from instinct. Certainly, education is the formation of the human being—and whoever says human being, says freedom.

Out of this arises the antinomy. How does one reconcile the presupposition of freedom being intrinsic to the student, and the intention of the educator to foster freedom, with the intervention of the educator in the personality of the student? The interposition of the educator means that the student will not be left to himself, to his own powers, but must encounter another different from himself. Education requires a duality: the educator and the student. It is the liberty of the student that suffers because of that duality, which implies limits, and thereby annuls the infinity in which true freedom consists. The student who finds himself confronted by a will stronger than his own to which he must submit, an intelligence armed by experience, that forestalls his own powers of observation and his zeal for his own experience, conceives the more powerful personality of the educator as a barrier that impedes the student's way toward a goal—toward which the student would have preferred to spontaneously and independently proceed—or he might imagine the educator providing a goal along a way that the student would have chosen of his own accord, along which he would have preferred to advance freely, joyfully, without compulsion. The student would have preferred to be left alone, to be free—as was God, when the world was not, and He created it out of nothing, by joyous *fiat*, symbol of the highest spiritual liberty.

For these considerations we have held that the major problem of education is that involving the relationship between the freedom of the student and the authority of the teacher. For that reason the great writers, who meditated on the questions of education, from Rousseau to Tolstoy, exalting the right of liberty, chose the extreme of denying the right of authority, to advocate a vague and intangible ideal of negative education.

We do not need to deny anything. We would construct rather than destroy. The school—this glorious legacy of human experience, this hearth which, throughout the millennia, has never been without the fire of the increasing human need to sublimate life through constant criticism and with inextinguishable love—may be transformed with time, but never destroyed. Let the schools remain, and let the teacher remain in his position, with his authority and with the limitations he places on the spontaneity and the liberty of the student. Those limitations, we would argue, are only apparent.

It is apparent if we are concerned with true education. A great injustice has weighed for centuries on the schools, viewed as prisons and places of torment, and on the teachers, scourged without pity by satirists as pedants. The schools have been charged with faults not of their own making, and teachers, genuine educators, have been identified as pedants—pedants who represent the very opposite of intelligent instruction and violative of every ethical inspiration of true educators, genuine teachers.

To determine whether education really limits the free activity of the student, it is ill-advised to observe any school whatever, in the abstract, which may or not be a school. Rather, one must examine an institution at that time when it succeeds in being a school, when the teacher teaches and the scholars learn. Such a time, even if only hypothetical, must be conceivable.

Let us imagine a teacher conducting lessons in Italian. The Italian language? Where is it to be found? In the grammar text or the dictionary? Yes—but only if the exposition of grammar can invest its rules with the vitality of examples of language spoken—and if the dictionary does not desiccate every word in the aridity of alphabetical abstraction—but employs the words in complete phrases, meaningful utterances of great authors or the common speech of the people. Only if the grammar text and the dictionary do not tear rules and words from the living body of language in which they originated and in which they will be joined again in the vibrancy of life and expressiveness. But more than in the grammar and the dictionary, language is in the writers themselves, now reading one and now another, each of whom knew how to most powerfully express our thoughts. The educator reads, and with him read the students. Thus they learn to know the language. They read Leopardi: the words of Leopardi, his soul, which with the reading of the teacher, expands throughout the school, combines in the soul of the students, quieting every other sentiment, and taking the place of any other thought. In each, the words of Leopardi throb, moves them, and arouses them. Each comes to know a Leopardi of his own, flesh of his flesh. In knowing his Leopardi the student experiences one of the finest moments of his life. His blood courses warm in his veins, and his life is full and made more lofty. Does anyone who hears within himself the echoes of the language of Leopardi, imagine that he hears the echo of an echo? The results of a language spoken after once spoken by the poet? Experience tells us that is not the case. Should anyone become distracted and no longer remain enraptured by the words of the poet, and imagine that the words they hear are not their own but those of the teacher, or rather, the words of the poet, they would be making a serious mistake—because that which is heard deep within oneself is one's own, entirely one's own. Leopardi cannot communicate poetry to those who cannot live in their own lives the love, and the intensity of sentiment of poetry. When they can so experience the poetry of Leopardi, Leopardi (or the teacher who presents him) no longer is a Leopardi materially external to the listener or the reader, but is his own Leopardi—the Leopardi he is able to fashion for himself. [In such circumstances,] the teacher is no longer external to the student. As St. Augustine long ago informed us, the teacher has become part of us.

He is within, even if we see him before us, there, at his lectern. Even there, he is part of us, object of our consciousness, uplifted within our soul, and possessed of our reverence, our faith, and our affection. He is *our* teacher, our very soul.

The duality of teacher and student is only apparent in education. First of all there is education, and then the antinomy makes its appearance. But the antinomy is resolved by education itself, from the moment that the teacher speaks the first word that reaches the soul of the student.

100 Origins and Doctrine of Fascism

The duality remains should the words of the teacher fail to reach the soul of the student. Under those circumstances, there is no education. But even under such circumstances, if the teacher is not completely inept, the barrier between the two works in favor of the spiritual development of the student. The ineptitude of the teacher, insufficient for the purposes of education, leads the student—motivated by the irrepressible liberty of his nature—to affirm his own personality with increased vigor. In spite of the inadequacies, or the intention, of the teacher, the school remains the hearth of liberty. A school that is not free, is an institution that is lifeless.

Index

action
  education and, 86
  Fascism and, 18, 34, 62
  problematic nature of, 86
  unity of thought and, 5, 22, 59
  will and, 82, 89
Alfieri, D., 4
anti-individualism, 34, 70
anti-intellectualism, 22–23
anti-materialism, 3, 6, 10, 12
anti-war movement in Italy, 2–3, 15, 18, 45
antinomy, of education, 88, 97, 99
Arais, Guido, 69
Aristotle, 78
Augustine, Saint, 99
authority
  liberty and, 30–31
  in nationalist States, 28
  respect for, needed, 17
  the State and, 30, 31, 32
  undermined in Italy, 15

Barone, D., 69
Bolshevism, Bolsheviks, 16, 19
brotherhood, 56
Byron, George Gordon, 24

Carl Albert, King of Sardinia and Piedmont, 72
Catholic Church, 6, 12, 13, 31–32
Cavour, Conte di, 4, 5, 6, 7
choice, 89, 93–94
ciphers, 80–81
class struggle, 59–60
cognition, 93
concrete personality, 77–78, 88
concrete will, 53–54
conscience, 92
consciousness
  freedom and, 93

  of nations, 54, 55
  self-control and, 79
  sensation and, 96
  of the State, 31, 54, 71
  will and, 54
constitution of Fascist Italy, 37–38, 40, 68, 72
contingencies, 95
Coppola (member Commission of XVIII), 69
corporativism, 29–30, 70–71
Corradini, Senator Enrico, 68
Crispi, Francesco, 8, 9
Croce, Benedetto, Fascism to, *xi*
culture
  anti-intellectualism and, 23
  of Fascism, 64–67
  of Italy, 43, 44, 48

Dalmatia, 2
De Sanctis, G., 11
Del Noce, Augusto, *ix*
delinquency, 91
democracy
  common denominator of, 61
  Fascist democracy, *xii*, 28–29
  liberal democracy, 60–62
  Wilson's brand of, 15
determinism, 91, 95
dictionaries, 98–99
directive minority, in Italy, *ix*, 1
duty, 60, 72, 92

education
  action and, 86
  antinomy of, 88, 97, 99
  failures in, 100
  in Fascist Italy, 28–29, 35, 41.n18, 52, 67
  in Italy, 9–10
  liberty and, 87–88, 97–98

personality and, 84–88
spirit and, 85, 86, 87–88
Ego, 77, 83
elites (the few), x, 4, 33
Epicureanism, of intellectualists, 23
ethical State, 34, 53–55, 56
evil, 90–91

faith, 65
Fascio di Combattimento, 18
Fascism, Fascists. *See also* Fascist Italy
  action and, 18, 34, 62
  anti-individualism of, 34, 70
  anti-intellectualism of, 22–23
  barbarism of, 52, 66
  to Croce, *xi*
  culture of, 64–67
  as a doctrine, *xi–xii, xiii,* 21–22, 24, 62, 64–65
  duty and, 60, 72, 92
  evolution of, 19–20, 24
  faith of, 65
  Fascist democracy, *xii,* 28–29
  freedom and, *xi–xii*
  Gentile's contribution to, *xi*
  history immanent in, 20
  ideas and, 18
  intellectualism rejected by, 33, 65–66
  liberalism compared to, 30–31, 54–55
  liberty and, *xi–xii,* 30–31
  Marxism-Leninism's affinities with, 74.n8
  Mazzini the master of, 60
  Mazzinianism and, *x–xi,* 21, 32
  a method, 24–25
  Mussolini on, *xiii.n6*
  nationalism and, 25, 27
  opponents of, 59–64
  Partito Nazionale Fascista (PNF), 68
  philosophy of, 33–35
  politics in, 24–25
  a religion, 56–57
  as a revolutionary State, 20
  Risorgimento and, *x–xi,* 48–49
  sacrifice and, 54, 60, 62, 72
  sentiment and, 21
  seriousness of, 57
  spirit of, 72
  the State and, 25–28, 34, 52–53, 70, 71–73
  style of, 34
  syndicalism's contribution to, 29, 59
  as a system, 18, 21–22, 24
  theory in, 23–24
  thought and, 21
  totalitarian character of, 20–21, 25, 40, 74.n10
  will and, 21, 66
  working classes and, 56
Fascist Italy
  action squads in, 19, 20, 49, 74.n7
  Catholic Church in, 31–32
  Commission of the XV, 68, 69
  Commission of the XVIII, 68–70, 72–73, 75.n12, 75.n13
  constitution of, 37–38, 40, 68, 72
  corporativism in, 29–30, 70–71
  as a democratic State, 28–29
  education in, 28–29, 35, 41.n18, 52, 67
  executive and legislative power in, 69–70
  Fasci, 19
  Fascio di Combattimento, 18
  Fascist Party structure, 20, 29
  the government in, 29
  immanentist character of, 32
  individuality of, 39–40
  law violations in, 19
  liberalism of, 31
  March on Rome (Oct 28, 1922), 19–20, 27, 51, 58, 74.n7
  Mazzinians' support for, 20
  monarchy in, 27, 38–39, 75.n12
  propaganda in, 21, 28–29
  revolution made by, *x–xi,* 18–19, 37–38, 40
  secret societies in, 68
  supporters within Italy, 20
  syndicates in, 29–30, 35, 68, 70
  values celebrated by, 35
  violence in, 20, 49–51, 58, 73.n2, 74.n8
Ferrari, Giuseppe, 6
force, 53, 63–64, 74.n7
Foscolo, Ugo, *ix,* 4
Franciscan benevolence, 50
free will, 89, 93–94
freedom
  consciousness and, 93
  Fascism and, *xi–xii*
  negation of, 94
  spirit and, 94, 97
  thought and, 97
Freemasonry, 13, 17, 46, 60

Index

Galileo, 78
Garibaldi, Giuseppe, 5
Gentile, Giovanni
   Commission of the XVIII member, 75.n13
   contribution to Fascism, *xiii*
   on heroes in history, *ix*
   individuals to, *xii*
   on Italy's involvement in First World War, *ix–x*
   Mazzini to, *x*
   as Minister of Education, 41.n8
   to Mussolini, *xii*
   Mussolini to, 32
   social change to, *ix–x*
Gini, Corrado, 69, 70
Gioberti, Vincenzo, *ix*, 4, 5, 6, 11
Giolitti, Giovanni, 14–16
Goethe, Johann Wolfgang von, 24
Grand Council of Fascism, 36–41

hatred, 90
heroes, *ix*

idealism, idealists, 5–7, 13
individualism, individualists
   anti-individualism, 34, 70
   Fascist opposition to, 34, 70
   of Italian Renaissance, 44
   of liberals, 10, 46
   materialism of, 10
   Mazzini on, 54–55
individuals
   goals to, 5
   and law, 8
   and liberty, 7
   and the State, 7–8, 25–26, 27–28, 29, 30, 31, 34–35, 61, 63
intellect, 66, 93
intellectualism, 22–23, 33, 65–66
intelligence, 55, 66
internationalism, Mussolini's opposition to, 17
interventionists, 2–3, 16, 17, 18
Italy. *See also* Fascist Italy; Mazzinianism; Risorgimento
   anti-war sentiment in post-war, 15
   authority undermined in, 15
   Bolshevism in, 16, 19
   Camera (lower house in Parliament), 61
   Catholicism in, 6, 12, 13
   culture of, 43, 44, 48
   diadochi in, 7
   directive minority in, *ix*, 1
   education in, 9–10
   essence of the nation of, 26
   First World War allies of, 15
   First World War dead, 57
   First World War involvement of, 2–3, 14–15, 49
   First World War veterans in, 16, 18–19, 20
   Franciscan benevolence in, 50
   a great power, 49
   intellectualism in, 65–66
   interventionists in, 2–3, 16, 17, 18
   the Left in, 7, 10
   Marxism in, 9–10
   Masonry (Freemasonry) in, 13, 46
   monarchy in, 26–27
   morality in, 10
   nationalism in, 13
   neutralists in, 2–3, 15, 18, 45
   old Italy, 44–46, 49
   Parliament in, 3
   patriotism in, 10
   positivism in, 10, 12
   post-First World War years in, 14–16, 18–19
   post-Risorgimento (demo-socialist) years in, 8–11
   pre-First World War spiritual crisis, 1–3, 14
   Quakerism in, 50
   redemption of, 18–19, 55–56, 59
   religion in, 6, 9
   Renaissance in, 43–44
   renewal in, feeling of, 13–14
   the Right in, 7, 13
   socialism, socialists in, 12, 13, 15
   Statuto of 1848, 36, 42.n18, 75.n12
   the two Italys, 44–46
   the two souls of, *x*, 2–3, 14
   working classes in, 9–10
   youth in, 11, 13–14, 16, 26, 45, 58

jargon, 80–81

Kant, Immanuel, 92

Lambruschini, R., 6
language, 79–81, 99
Lanza, D.S., 7

104   Origins of Fascism

Lanzillo, Agostino, 70
law
   essence of, 83
   Fascist violations of, 19
   force and, 53
   of the Grand Council of Fascism, 36–41
   individuals and, 8
   moral law, 92
   morality, religion subordinate to, 31
   Mussolini arbiter of, 36
   nations and, 18
   respect for, 17, 53
   sanctioned violence, 51
   the State and, 35, 82
   Statuto of 1848, 36, 42.n18, 75.n12
   transgressions of, 82, 83–84
   will and, 82
Leopardi, Giacomo, 4, 24, 99
Liberal Party, Italian, 60
liberalism, liberals
   Fascism compared to, 30–31, 54–55
   Franciscan benevolence of, 50
   individualism of, 10, 46
   Mazzini's characterization of, 53
   personality to, 54
   State and individuals to, 25, 29, 70
   types of, 62–63
   violence of, 50
liberty
   absoluteness of, 88
   authority and, 30–31
   education and, 87–88, 97–98
   Fascism and, *xi–xii*, 30–31
   force and, 63–64
   free will and, 89
   and immanence of State in individuals, 30
   to the Left, 7–8
   Mazzini on, 46
   moral obligation and, 92–93
   to the Right, 7–8
   spirit and, 92, 94–95
   the State and, 7–8, 9, 30, 34–35, 40
   thought and, 94
limits, 94–95
literati, 23

Machiavelli, Niccolò, 80
Manzoni, Alessandro, 4, 6, 24
Marinetti, Filippo Tommaso, 65
Marxism, 9–10, 12, 59–60

Marxism-Leninism, *xi–xii, xiii*, 74.n8
Masonry (Freemasonry), 13, 17, 46, 60
materialism
   anti-materialism, 3, 6, 10, 12
   freedom denied by, 94
   of individualists, 10
   of Leftists, 10
   of neutralists, 3
Mazzini, Giuseppe
   anti-materialism of, 10
   centrality to Fascism, 21, 32
   as exemplar, 14
   familiarity with, *ix*
   to Gentile, *x*
   on individualism, 54–55
   influence on Crispi, 8
   intellectuals and, 22
   liberalism characterized by, 53
   liberty and, 46
   master of Fascism, 60
   philosophy of, 24
   the Prophet, 57, 60
   rediscovered, 11
   religion of, 6
   Risorgimento and, 4
   unity of thought and action, 5
Mazzinianism
   concept of the nation in, 4–48
   development of, 5–6
   Fascism and, *x–xi*
   idealists and, 13
   the Left and, 10
   life viewed by, 60
   Mussolini and, *xi*
   nationalists and, 13
   politics in, 21
   syndicalists and, 13
   unity of thought and action, 5, 22
Mazzinians
   First World War veterans, 16
   Giolitti's opponents, 16
   Mussolini leader of, 16–17
   Risorgimento's leaders, 5
   support for Fascist Italy, 20
Mazziotti, M., 69
Melodia, Senator N., 68, 69
metaphysics, 10
Minghetti, Marco, 7
moral law, 92
morality, 10, 31, 54, 90–91
multitudes, *ix–x*
Mussolini, Benito, *Il Duce* (the Leader)

Index

allegiance to the King, 27, 75.n12
arbiter of law, 36
on Fascism, *xiii.n6*
to Gentile, 32
Gentile to, *xii*
leadership qualities, 14
Mazzinianism of, *xi*, 16–17
opponent of internationalism, 17
opponent of Masonry, 17
opponent of parliamentary reform, 17
sentiment preferred to precise doctrine, 65
socialist, 17
Sorellian syndicalism of, 17
a "tempist" (opportunist), 22, 24
veto power of, 75n12
violence and, 17

Napoleon III, 4
nationalism, nationalists
  authority to, 28
  Fascism and, 25, 27
  in Italy, 13
  monarchy to, 26–27
  nations to, 25–26, 28
  State and individual to, 25–26, 28
  targets of, 13
nation(s)
  concept of, 47–48
  consciousness of, 54, 55
  essence of the Italian nation, 26
  Fascist Party and the, 40
  ideal *vs.* actual, 35
  law and, 18
  as a mission, 47
  to nationalists, 25–26, 28
  States and, 17, 28, 52
  war as a binding element of, 2–3
naturalism, 26
nature, 96
neutralists, 2–3, 15, 18, 45

Panunzio, Sergio, 64–65
particularity, 78
personality
  concrete personality, 77–78, 88
  education and, 84–88
  essence of, 90
  as a foundation, 3
  history and, 47
  language and, 79–81

to liberals, 54
in old Italy, 46
particularity in, 78
the State and, 30, 34, 55
will and, 47
philosophy, 24, 33–35
Piccoli, D., 65
Plato, 82
politics, 33, 37
Popolari, 60
positivism, 10, 12
progress, 23
proletariat, syndicalism to, 12
pure syndicalism, 70–71

Quakerism, 50

reason, 90
redemption
  of humans, 91
  of Italy, 18–19, 55–56, 59
Risorgimento and, *x*
religion, 31
Ricasoli, Bettino, 6, 7
Rimini, Francesca da, 80
Risorgimento
  anti-materialism of, 6
  causal agent of, 4, 8
  elites in, 4
  Fascism and, *x–xi*, 48–49
  idealism of, 5–7
  literati and, 23
  and redemption of Italy, *x*
  unity of thought and action in, 5
  waning of, 7–11
Romagna, 17
Rosmini, Antonio, *ix*, 6, 11
Rossoni, Edmundo, 70
Rousseau, Jean-Jacques, 98

sacrifice, 54, 60, 62, 72
schools, 98, 100
science, 67
Sella, Quintino, 7
sensation, 96
sentiment, 21, 65, 90
Shelley, Percy Bysshe, 24
social change, *ix–x*
socialism, socialists
  individualism of, 10
  liberal democracy and, 60–62
  Mussolini's, 17

State and individual to, 25
syndicalism and, 12, 13
Socialist Party, Italian, 61–62
Socrates, 82
Sorel, Georges, 12
Sorellian syndicalism, 17, 58, 59
Spaventa, Bertrando, 11
spirit
   education and, 85, 86, 87–88
   of Fascism, 72
   freedom and, 94, 97
   language a product of, 80–81
   liberty and, 92, 94–95
   limits to, 95
   value entails, 31
the spiritual, 78
squadrism, 19, 20, 49, 74.n7
the State
   authority and, 30, 31, 32
   autonomy demonstrated by war, 53
   consciousness of, 31, 54, 71
   debasement of, 18
   the ethical State, 34, 53–55, 56
   Fascism a revolutionary, 20
   Fascist doctrine of, 25–28, 34, 52–53, 70, 71–73
   force employed by, 74.n7
   foundations of, 17–18
   the individual and, 7–8, 25–26, 27–28, 29, 30, 31, 34–35, 61, 63
   intelligence encompassed by, 55
   law and, 35, 82
   the Left and, 8
   to liberals, 25, 29, 70
   liberty and, 7–8, 9, 30, 34–35, 40
   the nation and, 17, 28, 52
   to nationalists, 25–26, 28
   nothing outside of, 40
   organic representation in, 30
   personality and, 30, 34, 55
   private initiative in, 82–83
   pure syndicalism and, 71
   to socialists, 25
   statolatry, 55–56
   the will of, 31, 35, 53, 84
Suvich, Fulvio, 69
syndicalism, syndicalists
   contribution to Fascism, 29, 59
   to Italian socialists, 12
   to the proletariat, 12
   pure syndicalism, 70–71
   Sorellian syndicalism, 17, 58, 59

targets of, 13
violence and, 12
syndicates
   in Fascist Italy, 29–30, 35, 68, 70
   in pure syndicalism, 71

teachers, 98–100
theory, 62
thought
   anti-intellectualism and, 22
   Fascism and, 21
   freedom and, 97
   liberation from, 88
   liberty and, 94
   philosophies in bodies of, 24
   reality embodied within, 96
   responsibility for, 93
   unity of action and, 5, 22, 59
Tolstoy, Leo, 98
Tommaseo, Niccolò, 6
totalitarianism, Fascism and, 20–21, 25, 40, 74.n10
Trento, 2
Treves, Claudio, 18
Trieste, 2
trigonometry, 22
truncheon, as a moral force, 64, 74.n7
truth, 58, 93, 94
Turati, Filippo, 18

Ugolino, Count of Pisa, 80
Umberto I, King of Italy, 8, 11

values, 3, 31, 35
velleities, 82, 83
Vico, Giambatista, 11, 51–52
violence
   in Fascist Italy, 20, 49–51, 58, 73.n2, 74.n8
   in humans, 89
   of liberals, 50
   Mussolini and, 17
   sanctioned, 51
   syndicalism and, 12
Vittorio Emanuele III, King of Italy, 3, 5, 27
Vittorio Veneto, battle of, 27
volition, 95

war, 2–3, 23, 53
will
   action and, 82, 89

concrete will, 53–54
consciousness and, 54
Fascism and, 21, 66
intellect and, 93
intelligence and, 66
of Italian nation, 18–19
law and, 82
nationality and, 81
personality and, 47
of Risorgimento's leaders, 4
a shared entity, 81–82, 83–84
of the State, 31, 35, 53, 84
values determined by, 3
Wilson, Woodrow, 15